*Engraved for Headleys Illustrated Life and Travels of General Grant.
From a Photograph by Brady.*

H.B. Hall & Sons N.Y.

REPORT

OF

LIEUTENANT GENERAL U. S. GRANT,

OF THE

ARMIES OF THE UNITED STATES
1864 -1865.

Submitted

Headquarters Armies of the United States

Washington D.C. July 22, 1865

Large print hardcover
ISBN   9781582188607

Large print paperback
ISBN 9781582188614

Published July 2020

River-
Moor
Books

www.RiverMoorBooks.com
Scituate, Massachusetts

River-Moor Books is an imprint of Digital Scanning Inc., reproducing
Large Print Editions of significantly relevant titles pertaining to United
States History.

Preface

This report submitted by U.S. Grant in the summer of 1865 describes the events starting in the spring of 1864 to the conclusion and surrendering of Robert E. Lee at Appomattox.

Through a series of dispatches and letters to his command staff General Grant describes his decisions and logic as he executes the final battles to end the war. His narrative and concise clarity describe his strategic thinking, battle tactics and vision for ending the war.

Throughout the report Grant shows a determined nature in his unyielding march forward to end the insurrection with the final objective of forcing the south to surrender.

Table of Contents

REPORT

OF

LIEUTENANT General U.S. Grant

REPORT

OF

LIEUTENANT GENERAL U. S. GRANT,

OF THE

ARMIES OF THE UNITED STATES – 1864-'65.

HEADQUARTERS ARMIES OF THE UNITED STATES,
Washington, D. C., July 22, 1865.

SIR: I have the honor to submit the following report of the operations of the armies of the United States from the date of my appointment to command the same:

From an early period in the rebellion I had been impressed with the idea that active and continuous operations of all the troops that could be brought into the field, regardless of season and weather, were necessary to a speedy termination of the war. The resources of the enemy and his numerical strength were far inferior to ours; but as an offset to this, we had a vast territory with a population hostile to the government, to garrison, and long lines of river and railroad communications to protect, to enable us to supply the operating armies.

The armies in the east and west acted independently and without concert, like a balky team, no two ever pulling together, enabling the enemy to use to great advantage his interior lines of communication for transporting troops from east to west, re-enforcing the army most vigorously pressed, and to furlough large numbers, during seasons of inactivity on our part, to go to their homes and do the work of producing for the support of their armies. It was a question whether our numerical strength and resources were not more than balanced by these disadvantages and the enemy's superior position.

From the first, I was firm in the conviction that no peace could be had that would be stable and conducive to the happiness of the people, both north and south, until the military power of the rebellion was entirely broken.

I therefore determined, first, to use the greatest number of troops practicable against the armed force of the enemy; preventing him from using the same force at different seasons against first one and then another of our armies, and the possibility of repose for refitting and producing necessary supplies for carrying on resistance. Second, to hammer continuously against, the armed force of the enemy and his resources, until by mere attrition, if in no other way, there should be nothing left to him but an equal submission with the loyal section of our common country to the Constitution and laws of the land.

These views have been kept constantly in mind, and orders given and campaigns made to carry them out. Whether they might have been better in conception and execution is for the people, who mourn the loss of friends fallen, and who have to pay the pecuniary cost, to say. All I can say is, that what I have done has been done conscientiously, to the best of my ability, and in what I conceived to be for the best interests of the whole country.

At the date when this report begins the situation of the contending forces was about as – follows: The Mississippi river was strongly garrisoned by federal troops from St. Louis, Missouri, to its mouth. The line of the Arkansas was also held, thus giving us armed possession of all west of the Mississippi, north of that stream. A few points in southern Louisiana, not remote from the river, were held by us, together with small garrison at and near the mouth of the Rio Grande. All the balance of the vast territory of Arkansas, Louisiana, and Texas was in the almost undisputed possession of the enemy, with an army of probably not less than 80,000 effective men that could have been brought into the field had there been sufficient opposition to have brought them out. The let-alone policy had demoralized this force so that probably but little more than one-half of it was ever present in garrison at any one time. But, the one-half, or 40,000 men, with the bands of guerillas scattered through Missouri, Arkansas, and along the Mississippi river, and the disloyal character of much of the population, compelled the use of a large number of troops to keep navigation open on the river, and to protect the loyal people to the west of it. To the east of the Mississippi we held substantially with the line of the Tennessee and Holston rivers, running eastward to include nearly all of the State of Tennessee. South of Chattanooga a small foothold had been obtained in Georgia, sufficient to protect East Tennessee from incursions from the enemy's force at Dalton, Georgia. West Virginia was substantially within our lines. Virginia, with the exception of the northern border, the Potomac river, a small area about the mouth of James river covered by the troops at Norfolk and Fort Monroe, and the territory covered by the army of the Potomac lying along the Rapidan, was in the possession of the enemy. Along the sea-coast footholds had been obtained at

Plymouth, Washington, and Newbern, in North Carolina; Beaufort, Folly and Morris Island, Hilton Head, Fort Pulaski, and Port Royal in South Carolina; Fernandina and St. Augustine, in Florida. Key West and Pensacola were also in our possession, while all the important ports were blockaded by the navy. The accompanying map, a copy of which was sent to General Sherman and other commanders in March, 1864, shows by red lines the territory occupied by us at the beginning of the rebellion and at the opening of the campaign of 1864, while those in blue are the lines which it was proposed to occupy.

Behind the Union lines there were many bands of guerillas and a large population disloyal to the government, making it necessary to guard every foot of road or river used in supplying our armies. In the south a reign of military despotism prevailed, which made every man and boy capable of bearing arms a soldier, and those who could not bear arms in the field acted as provosts for collecting deserters and returning them. This enabled the enemy to bring almost his entire strength into the field.

The enemy had concentrated the bulk of his forces east of the Mississippi into two armies, commanded by Generals R. E. Lee and J. E. Johnston, his ablest and best generals. The army commanded by Lee occupied the south bank of the Rapidan, extending from Mine Run westward, strongly intrenched, covering and defending Richmond, the rebel capital, against the army of the Potomac. The army under Johnston occupied a strongly intrenched position at Dalton, Georgia, covering and defending Atlanta, Georgia, a place of great importance as a railroad centre, against the armies under Major General W. T. Sherman. In addition to these armies, he had a large cavalry force under Forrest, in northeast Mississippi, a considerable force, of all arms, in the

Shenandoah valley, and in the western part of Virginia and extreme eastern part of Tennessee; and also confronting our sea-coast garrisons, and holding blockaded ports where we had no foothold upon land.

These two armies, and the cities covered and defended by them, were the main objective points of the campaign.

Major General W. T. Sherman, who was appointed to the command of the military division of the Mississippi, embracing all the armies and territory east of the Mississippi river to the Alleghanies, and the department of Arkansas, west of the Mississippi, had the immediate command of the armies operating against Johnston.

Major General George G. Meade had the immediate command of the army of the Potomac, from where I exercised general supervision of the movements of all our armies.

General Sherman was instructed to move against Johnston's army, to break it up, and to go into the interior of the enemy's country as far as he could, inflicting all the damage he could upon their war resources. If the enemy in his front showed signs of joining Lee, to follow him up to the full extent of his ability, while I would prevent the concentration of Lee upon him if it was in the power of the army of the Potomac to do so. More specific written instructions were not given, for the reason that I had talked over with him the plans of the campaign, and was satisfied that he understood them and would execute them to the fullest extent possible.

Major General N. P. Banks, then on an expedition up Red river against Shreveport, Louisiana, (which had been organized previous to my appointment to command,) was notified by me on the 15th of March of the importance it was that Shreveport should be taken at the earliest possible day, and that if he found that the taking of it would occupy from ten to fifteen days' more time than General Sherman had given his troops to be absent from their command, he would send them back at the time specified by General Sherman, even if it led to the abandonment of the main object of the Red river expedition, for this force was necessary to movements east of the Mississippi; that should his expedition prove successful, he would hold Shreveport and the Red river with such force as he might deem necessary, and return the balance of his troops to the neighborhood of New Orleans, commencing no move for the further acquisition of territory unless it was to make that then held by him more easily held; that it might be a part of the spring campaign to move against Mobile; that it certainly would be if troops enough could be obtained to make it without embarrassing other movements; that New Orleans would be the point of departure for such an expedition; also, that I had directed General Steele to make a real move from Arkansas, as suggested by him, (General Banks,) instead of a demonstration, as Steele thought advisable.

On the 21st of March, in addition to the foregoing notification and directions, he was instructed as follows:

"1st. If successful in your expedition against Shreveport, that you turn over the defence of the Red river to General Steele and the navy.

"2d. That you abandon Texas entirely with the exception of your hold upon the Rio Grande. This can be held with four thousand men, if they will turn their attention immediately to for-tifying their positions. At least one-half of the force required for this service might be taken from the colored troops.

"3d. By properly fortifying on the Mississippi river, the force to guard it from Port Hudson to New Orleans can be reduced to ten thousand men, if not to a less number. Six thousand more would then hold all the rest of the territory necessary to hold until active operations can be resumed west of the river. According to your last return this would give you a force of over thirty thousand effective men with which to move against Mobile. To this I expect to add five thousand men from Missouri. If, however, you think the force here stated too small to hold the territory regarded as necessary to hold possession of, I would say, concentrate at least twenty-five thousand men of your present command for operations against Mobile. With these and such additions as I can give you from elsewhere, lose no time in making a demonstration, to be followed by an attack upon Mobile. Two or more iron-clads will be ordered to report to Admiral Farragut. This gives him a strong naval fleet with which to cooperate. You can make your own arrangements with the Admiral for his cooperation, and select your own line of approach. My own idea of the matter is that Pascagoula should be your base, but, from your long service in the Gulf department, you will know best about the matter. It is intended that your movements shall be cooperative with movements elsewhere, and you cannot now start too soon. All I would now add is, that you commence the concentration of your forces at once. Preserve a profound secrecy of what you intend doing, and start at the earliest possible moment.

"U. S. GRANT, Lieutenant General.

"Major General N. P. BANKS."

Major General Meade was instructed that Lee's army would be his objective point; that wherever Lee went he would go also.

For his movement two plans presented themselves: One to cross the Rapidan below Lee, moving by his right flank; the other above, moving by his left. Each presented advantages over the other, with corresponding objections. By crossing above, Lee would be cut off from all chance of ignoring Richmond or going north on a raid. But if we took this route all we did would have to be done whilst the rations we started with held out; besides, it separated us from Butler, so that he could not be directed how to co-operate. If we took the other route, Brandy Station could be used as a base of supplies until another was secured on the York or James rivers. Of these, however, it was decided to take the lower route.

The following letter of instruction was addressed to Major General B. F. Butler:

"FORT MONROE, VA., April 2, 1864.

"GENERAL; In the spring campaign, which it is desirable shall commence at as early a day as practicable, it is proposed to have cooperative action of all the armies in the field, as far as this object can be accomplished.

"It will not be possible to unite our armies into two or three large ones to act as so many units, owing to the absolute necessity of holding on to the territory already taken from the enemy. But, generally speaking, concentration can be practically effected by armies moving to the interior of the enemy's country from the territory they have to guard. By such movement they interpose themselves between the enemy and the country to be guarded, thereby reducing the number necessary to guard important points, or at least occupy the attention of a part of the enemy's force, if no greater object is gained. Lee's army and Richmond being the greater objects towards which our attention must be directed in the next campaign, it is desirable to unite all the force we can against them. The necessity of covering Washington with the army of the Potomac, and of covering your department with your army, makes it impossible to unite these forces at the beginning of any move. I propose, therefore, what comes nearest this of anything that seems practicable: The army of the Potomac will act from its present base, Lee's army being the objective point. You will collect all the forces from your command that can be spared from garrison duty – I should say not less than twenty thousand effective men – to operate on the south side of James river, Richmond being your objective point. To the force you already have will be added about ten thousand men from South Carolina, under Major General Gillmore, who will command them in person. Major General W. F. Smith is ordered to report to you, to command the troops sent into the field from your own department.

"General Gillmore will be ordered to report to you at Fortress Monroe, with all the troops on transports, by the 38th instant, or as soon thereafter as practicable. Should you not receive notice by that time to move, you will make such disposition of them and your other forces as you may deem best calculated to deceive the enemy as to the real move to be made.

"When you are notified to move take City Point with as much force as possible. Fortify or rather intrench, at once, and concentrate all your troops for the field there as rapidly as you can. From City Point directions cannot be given at this time for your further movements.

"The fact that has already been stated – that is, that Richmond is to be your objective point and that there is to be co-operation between your force and the army of the Potomac – must be your guide. This indicates the necessity of your holding close to the south bank of the James river as you advance. Then, should the enemy be forced into his intrenchments in Richmond, the army of the Potomac would follow, and by means of transports the two armies would become a unit.

"All the minor details of your advance are left entirely to your direction. If, however you think it practicable to use your cavalry south of you so as to cut the railroad about Hick's ford about the time of the general advance, it would be of immense advantage.

"You will please forward for my information, at the earliest practicable day, all orders details and instructions you may give for the execution of this order.

"U. S. GRANT, Lieutenant General.

"Major General B. F. BUTLER."

On the 16th, these instructions were substantially reiterated. On the 19th, in order to secure full co-operation between his army and that of General Meade, he was informed that I expected him to move from Fort Monroe the same day that General Meade moved from Culpeper. The exact time I was to telegraph him as soon as it was fixed, and that it would not be earlier than the 27th of April; that it was my intention to fight Lee between Culpeper and Richmond if he would stand. Should he, however, fall back into Richmond, I would follow up and make a junction with his (General Butler's) army on the James river; that, could I be certain he would be able to invest Richmond on the south side so as to have his left resting on the James, above the city, I would form the junction there; that circumstances might make this course advisable anyhow; that he should use every exertion to secure footing as far up the south side of the river as he could, and as soon as possible after the receipt of orders to move; that if he could not carry the city, he should at least detain as large a force as possible.

In cooperation with the main movements against Lee and Johnston, I was desirous of using all other troops necessarily kept in departments remote from the fields of immediate operations, and also those kept in the background for the protection of our extended lines between the loyal States and the armies operating against them.

A very considerable force under command of Major General Sigel was so held for the protection of West Virginia, and the frontiers of Maryland and Pennsylvania. Whilst these troops could not be withdrawn to distant fields without exposing the north to invasion by comparatively small bodies of the enemy, they could act directly to their front and give better protection than if lying idle in garrison. By such movement they would either compel the enemy to detach largely for the protection of his supplies and lines of communication, or he would lose them.

General Sigel was therefore directed to organize all his available force into two expeditions, to move from Beverly and Charleston, under command of Generals Ord and Crook, against the East Tennessee and Virginia railroad. Subsequently, General Ord having been relieved at his own request, General Sigel was instructed, at his own suggestion, to give up the expedition by Beverly and to form two columns, one under General Crook, on the Kanawha, numbering about ten thousand men, and one on the Shenandoah, numbering about seven thousand men. The one on the Shenandoah to assemble between Cumberland and the Shenandoah, and the infantry and artillery advanced to Cedar creek with such cavalry as could be made available at the moment, to threaten the enemy in the Shenandoah valley, and advance as far as possible; while General Crook would take possession of Lewisburg with part of his force and move down the Tennessee railroad, doing as much damage as he could, destroying the New river bridge and the salt-works at Saltville, Va.

Owing to the weather and bad condition of the roads, operations were delayed until the 1st of May, when, everything being in readiness and the roads favorable, orders were given for a general movement of all the armies not later than the 4th of May.

My first, object being to break the military power of the rebellion and capture the enemy's important strongholds, made me desirous that General Butler should succeed in his movement against Richmond, as that would tend more than anything else, unless it were the capture of Lee's army, to accomplish this desired result in the east. If he failed, it was my determination, by hard fighting, either to compel Lee to retreat or to so cripple him that he could not detach a large force to go north and still retain enough for the defence of Richmond. It was well understood, by both Generals Butler and Meade, before starting on the campaign, that it was my intention to put both their armies south of the James river, in case of failure to destroy Lee without it.

Before giving General Butler his instructions, I visited him at Fort Monroe, and in conversation pointed out the apparent importance of getting possession of Petersburg and destroying railroad communication as far south as possible. Believing, however, in the practicability of capturing Richmond unless it was re-enforced, I made that the objective point of his operations. As the army of the Potomac was to move simultaneously with him, Lee could not detach from his army with safety, and the enemy did not have troops elsewhere to bring to the defence of the city in time to meet a rapid movement from the north of James river.

I may here state that, commanding all the armies as I did, I tried, as far as possible, to leave General Meade in independent command of the army of the Potomac. My instructions for that army were all through him, and were general in their nature, leaving all the details and the execution to him. The campaigns that followed proved him to be the right man in the right place. His commanding always in the presence of an officer, superior to him in rank, has drawn from him much of that public attention that his zeal and ability entitle him to, and which he would otherwise have received.

The movement of the army of the Potomac commenced early on the morning of the 4th of May, under the immediate direction and orders of Major General Meade, pursuant to instructions. Before night the whole army was across the Rapidan, (the 5th and 6th corps crossing at Germania ford, and the 2d corps at United States ford, the cavalry, under Major General Sheridan, moving in advance,) with the greater part of its trains, numbering about 4,000 wagons, meeting with but slight opposition. The average distance traveled by the troops that day was about twelve miles. This I regarded as a great success, and it removed from my mind the most serious apprehensions I had entertained, that of crossing the river in the face of an active, large, well-appointed and ably-commanded army, and how so large a train was to be carried through a hostile country and protected. Early on the 5th, the advance corps (the 5th, Major General G. K. Warren commanding) met and engaged the enemy outside his entrenchments near Mine Run. The battle raged furiously all day, the whole army being brought into the fight as fast as the corps could be got upon the field, which, considering the density of the forest and narrowness of the roads, was done with commendable promptness.

General Burnside, with the 9th corps, was, at the time the army of the Potomac moved, left with the bulk of his corps at the crossing of the Rappahannock river and Alexandria railroad, holding the road back to Bull Run, with instructions not to move until he received notice that a crossing of the Rapidan was secured, but to move promptly as soon as such notice was received. This crossing he was apprised of on the afternoon of the 4th. By six o'clock of the morning of the 6th he was leading his corps into action near the Wilderness tavern, some of his troops having marched a distance of over thirty miles, crossing both the Rappahannock and Rapidan rivers. Considering that a large proportion, probably two-thirds of his command, was composed of new troops, unaccustomed to marches and carrying the accoutrements of a soldier, this was a remarkable march.

The battle of the Wilderness was renewed by us at five o'clock on the morning of the 6th, and continued with unabated fury until darkness set in, each army holding substantially the same position that they had on the evening of the 5th. After dark the enemy made a feeble attempt to turn our right Bank, capturing several hundred prisoners and creating considerable confusion. But the promptness of General Sedgwick, who was personally present and commanded that part of our line, soon reformed it and restored order. On the morning of the 7th reconnaissances showed that the enemy had fallen behind his intrenched lines, with pickets to the front, covering a part of the battlefield. From this it was evident to my mind that the two days' fighting had satisfied him of his inability to further maintain the contest in the open field, notwithstanding his advantage of position, and that he would wait an attack behind his works. I therefore determined to push on and put my whole force between him and Richmond; and orders were at once issued for a movement by his right flank. On the night of the 7th the march was commenced towards Spottsylvania Court-House, the 5th corps moving on the most direct road. But the enemy having become apprised of our movement, and having the shorter line, was enabled to reach there first. On the 8th, General Warren met a force of the enemy which had been sent out to oppose and delay his advance, to gain time to fortify the line taken up at Spottsylvania. This force was steadily driven back on the main force, within the recently constructed works, after con-siderable fighting, resulting in severe loss to both sides. On the morning of the 9th General Sheridan started on a raid against the enemy's lines of communication with Richmond. The 9th, 10th, and 11th were spent in maneuvering and fighting, without decisive results. Among the killed on the 9th was that able and distinguished soldier Major General John Sedgwick, commanding the 6th army corps. Major General H. G. Wright succeeded him in command. Early on the morning of the 12th a general attack was made on the enemy in position. The 2d corps, Major General Hancock commanding, carried a salient of his line, capturing most of Johnston's division of Ewell's corps and twenty pieces of ar-tillery. But the resistance was so obstinate that the advantage gained did not prove decisive. The 13th, 14h, 15th, 16th, 17th, and 18th, were consumed in maneuvering and awaiting the arrival of re-enforcements from Washington. Deeming it impracticable to make any further attack upon the enemy at Spottsylvania Court-House, orders were issued on the 18th with a view to a movement to the North Anna, to commence at 12 o'clock on the night of the 19th. Late in the afternoon of the 19th Ewell's corps came out of its works on our extreme right flank; but the attack was promptly repulsed, with heavy loss. This delayed the movement to the North Anna until the night of the 21st, when it was commenced. But the enemy again having the shorter line, and being in possession of the main roads, was enabled to reach the North Anna in advance of us, and took position behind it. The 5th corps reached the North Anna on the afternoon of the 23d, closely followed by the 6th corps. The 2d and 9th corps got up about the same time, the 2d holding the railroad bridge and the 9th lying between that and Jericho ford. General Warren effected a crossing the same afternoon, and got a position without much opposition. Soon after getting into position he was violently attacked, but repulsed the enemy with great slaughter. On the 25th General Sheridan rejoined the army of the Potomac from the raid on which he started from Spottsylvania, having destroyed the depots at Beaver Dam and Ashland stations, four trains of cars, large supplies of rations, and many miles of railroad track; recaptured about four hundred of our men, on their way to Richmond as prisoners of war; met and defeated the enemy's cavalry at Yellow Tavern; carried the first line of works around. Richmond, (but finding the second line too strong to be carried by assault) re-crossed to the north bank of the Chickahominy at Meadow's Bridge, under heavy fire, and moved by a detour to Haxall's landing, on the James river, where he communicated with General Butler. This raid had the effect of drawing off the whole of the enemy's cavalry force, and making it comparatively easy to guard our trains.

General Butler moved his main force up the James river, in pursuance of instructions, on the 4th of May, General Gillmore having joined him with the 10th corps. At the same time he sent a force of 1,800 cavalry, by way of West Point, to form a junction with him wherever he might get a foothold, and a force of 3,000 cavalry, under General Kautz, from Suffolk, to operate against the roads south of Petersburg and Richmond. On the 5th he occupied, without opposition, both City Point and Bermuda Hundred, his movement being a complete surprise. On the 6th he was in position with his main army, and commenced intrenching. On the 7th he made a reconnaissance against the Petersburg and Richmond railroad, destroying a portion of it after some fighting. On the 9th he telegraphed as follows:

"HEADQUARTERS NEAR BERMUDA LANDING,
May 9, 1864

"Our operations may be summed up in a few words. With 1,700 cavalry we have advanced up the Peninsula, forced the Chickahominy, and have safely brought them to our present position. These were colored cavalry, and are now holding our advance pickets towards Richmond.

"General Kautz with three thousand cavalry from Suffolk, on the same day with our movement up James river, forced the Blackwater, burned the railroad bridge at Stony creek, below Petersburg, cutting in two Beauregard's force at that point.

"We have landed here, intrenched ourselves, destroyed many miles of railroad, and got a position which with proper supplies we can hold out against the whole of Lee's army. I have ordered up the supplies.

Beauregard with a large portion of his force was left south by the cutting of the railroads by Kautz. That portion which reached Petersburg under Hill I have whipped today, killing and wounding many and taking many prisoners, after a severe and well contested fight.

"General Grant will not be troubled with any further reinforcements to Lee from Beauregard's force.

"BENJAMIN F. BUTLER.

"Major General.

"Hon. E. M. STANTON, Secretary of War."

On the evening of the 13th and morning of the 14th he carried a portion of the enemy's first line of defences at Drury's Bluff, or Fort Darling, with small loss. The time thus consumed from the 6th lost to us the benefit of the surprise and capture of Richmond and Petersburg, enabling, as it did, Beauregard to collect his loose forces in North and South Carolina and bring them to the define of those places. On the 16th the enemy attacked General Butler in his position in front of Drury's Bluff. He was forced back, or drew back, into his intrenchments between the forks of the James and Appomattox rivers, the enemy intrenching strongly in his front, thus covering his railroads, the city, and all that was valuable to him. His army, therefore, though in a position of great security, was as completely shut off from further operations directly against Richmond as if it had been in a bottle strongly corked. It required but a comparatively small force of the enemy to hold it there.

On the 12th General Kautz with his cavalry was started on a raid against the Danville railroad, which he struck at Coalfield, Powhatan, and Chola stations, destroying them, the railroad track, two freight trains, and one locomotive, together with large quantities of commissary and other stores; thence crossing to the South Side road, struck it at Wilson's, Wellsville, and Black and White stations, destroying the road and station-houses; thence he proceeded to City Point, which he reached on the 18th.

On the 19th of April, and prior to the movement of General Butler, the enemy, with a land force under General Hoke and an iron-clad ram, attacked Plymouth, N. C., commanded by General H. W. Wessels, and our gunboats there, and after severe fighting the place was carried by assault and the entire garrison and armament captured. The gunboat Smithfield was sunk and the Miami disabled.

The army sent to operate against Richmond having hermetically sealed itself up at Bermuda Hundred, the enemy was enabled to bring the most if not all the re-enforcements brought from the south by Beauregard against the army of the Potomac. In addition to this re-enforcement, a very considerable one, probably not less than 15,000 men, was obtained by calling in the scattered troops under Breckinridge from the western part of Virginia.

The position at Bermuda Hundred was as easy to defend as it was difficult to operate from against the enemy. I determined, therefore, to bring from it all available forces, leaving enough only to secure what had been gained, and accordingly, on the 22d, I directed that they be sent forward, under command of Major General W. F. Smith, to join the army of the Potomac.

On the 24th of May the 9th army corps, commanded by Major General A. E. Burnside, was assigned to the army of the Potomac, and from this time forward constituted a portion of Major General Meade's command.

Finding the enemy's position the North Anna stronger than either of his previous ones, I withdrew on the night of the 26th to the north bank of the North Anna, and moved via Hanovertown to turn the enemy's position by his right.

Generals Torbert's and Merritt's divisions of cavalry, under Sheridan, and the 6th corps led the advance; crossed the Pamunky river at Hanovertown after considerable fighting, and on the 28th the two divisions of cavalry had a severe but successful engagement with the enemy at Haw's shop. On the 29th and 30th we advanced, with heavy skirmishing, to the Hanover Court House and Cold Harbor road, and developed the enemy's position north of the Chickahominy. Late on the evening of the last day the enemy came out and attacked our left, but was repulsed with very considerable loss. An attack was immediately ordered by General Meade along his whole line, which resulted in driving the enemy from a part of his intrenched skirmish line.

On the 31st General Wilson's division of cavalry destroyed the railroad bridges over the South Anna river, after defeating the enemy's cavalry. General Sheridan, on the same day, reached Cold Harbor, and held it until relieved by the 6th corps and General Smith's command, which had just arrived, via White House, from General Butler's army.

On the 1st day of June an attack was made at 5 p. m. by the 6th corps and the troops under General Smith, the other corps being held in readiness to advance on the receipt of orders. This resulted in our carrying and holding the enemy's first line of works in front of the right of the 6th corps and in front of General Smith. During the attack the enemy made repeated assaults on each of the corps not engaged in the main attack, but were repulsed with heavy loss in every instance. That night he made several assaults to regain what he had lost in the day, but failed. The 2d was spent in getting troops into position for an attack on the 3d. On the 3d of June we again assaulted the enemy's works, in the hope of driving him from his position. In this attempt our loss was heavy, while that of the enemy, I have reason to believe, was comparatively light. It was the only general attack made from the Rapidan to the James which did not inflict upon the enemy losses to compensate for our own losses. I would not be understood as saying that all previous attacks resulted in victories to our arms, or accomplished as much as I had hoped from them; but they inflicted upon the enemy severe losses, which tended, in the end, to the complete overthrow of the rebellion.

From the proximity of the enemy to his defences around Richmond, it was impossible by any flank movement to interpose between him and the city. I was still in a condition to either move by his left flank and invest Richmond from the north side, or continue my move by his right flank to the south side of the James. While the former might have been better as a covering for Washington, yet a full survey of all the ground satisfied me that it would be impracticable to hold a line north and east of Richmond that would protect the Fredericksburg railroad – a long, vulnerable line, which would exhaust much of our strength to guard, and that would have to be protected to supply the army, and would leave open to the enemy all his lines of communication on the south side of the James. My idea, from the start, had been to beat Lee's army north of Richmond if possible. Then, after destroying his lines of communication north of the James river, to transfer the army to the south side and besiege Lee in Richmond, or follow him south if he should retreat. After the battle of the Wilderness it was evident that the enemy deemed it of the first importance to run no risks with the army he then had. He acted purely on the defensive behind breastworks, or feebly on the offensive immediately in front of them, and where, in case of repulse, he could easily retire behind them. Without a greater sacrifice of life than I was willing to make, all could not be accomplished that I had designed north of Richmond. I therefore determined to continue to hold substantially the ground we then occupied, taking advantage of any favorable circumstances that might present themselves, until the cavalry could be sent to Charlottesville and Gordonsville, to effectually break up the railroad connexion between Richmond and the Shenandoah valley and Lynchburg; and, when the cavalry got well off, to move the army to the south side of the James river, by the enemy's right flank, where I felt I could cut off all his sources of supply except by the canal.

On the 7th two divisions of cavalry, under General Sheridan, got off on the expedition against the Virginia Central railroad, with instructions to Hunter, whom I hoped be would meet near Charlottesville, to join his forces to Sheridan's, and after the work laid out for them was thoroughly done, to join the army of the Potomac by the route laid down in Sheridan's instructions.

On the 10th of June General Butler sent a force of infantry under General Gillmore, and cavalry under General Kautz, to capture Petersburg if possible, and destroy the railroad and common bridges across the Appomattox. The cavalry carried the works on the south side, and penetrated well in towards the town, but were forced to retire. General Gillmore finding the works which he approached very strong, and deeming an assault impracticable, returned to Bermuda Hundred without attempting one.

Attaching great importance to the possession of Petersburg, I sent back to Bermuda Hundred and City Point General Smith's command by water, via the White House, to reach there in advance of the army of the Potomac. This was for the express purpose of securing Petersburg before the enemy, becoming aware of our intention, could re-enforce the place.

The movement from Cold Harbor commenced after dark on the evening of the 12th; one division of cavalry, under General Wilson, and the 5th corps crossed the Chickahominy at Long Bridge, and moved out to White Oak swamp, to cover the crossings of the other corps. The advance corps reached James river, at Wilcox's landing and Charles City Court House, on the night of the 13th.

During three long years the armies of the Potomac and northern Virginia had been confronting each other. In that time they had fought more desperate battles than it probably ever before fell to the lot of two armies to fight, without materially changing the vantage-ground of either. The southern press and people, with more shrewdness than was displayed in the north, finding that they had failed to capture Washington and march on to New York, as they had boasted they would do, assumed that they only defended their capital and southern territory. Hence, Antietam, Gettysburg, and all the other battles that had been fought, were by them set down as failures on our part, and victories for them. Their army believed this. It produced a morale which could only be overcome by desperate and continuous hard fighting. The battles of the Wilderness, Spottsylvania, North Anna, and Cold Harbor, bloody and terrible as they were on our side, were even more damaging to the enemy, and so crippled him as to make him wary ever after of taking the offensive. His losses in men were probably not so great, owing to the fact that we were, save in the Wilderness, almost invariably the attacking party; and when he did attack it was in the open field. The details of these battles, which for endurance and bravery on the part of the soldiery have rarely been surpassed, are given in the report of Major General Meade, and the subordinate reports accompanying it.

During the campaign of forty-three days, from the Rapidan to James river, the army had to be supplied from an ever-shifting base, by wagons, over narrow roads, through a densely wooded country, with a lack of wharves at each new base from which to conveniently discharge vessels. Too much credit cannot, therefore, be awarded to the quartermaster and commissary departments for the zeal and efficiency displayed by them. Under the general supervision of the chief quartermaster, Brigadier General R. Ingalls, the trains were made to occupy all the available roads between the army and our water base, and but little difficulty was experienced in protecting them.

The movement of the Kanawha and Shenandoah valleys, under General Sigel, commenced on the first of May. General Crook, who had the immediate command of the Kanawha expedition, divided his forces into two columns, giving one, composed of cavalry, to General Averill. They crossed the mountains by separate routes. Averill struck the Tennessee and Virginia railroad, near Wytheville, on the 10th, and proceeding to New river and Christiansburg, destroyed the road, several important bridges and depots, including New river Bridge, forming a junction with Crook at Union on the 15th. General Sigel moved up the Shenandoah Valley, met the enemy at New Market on the 15th and, after a severe engagement, was defeated with heavy loss, and retired behind Cedar creek. Not regarding the operations of General Sigel as satisfactory, I asked his removal from command, and Major General Hunter was appointed to supersede him. His instructions were embraced in the following despatches to Major General H. W. Halleck, chief of staff of the army:

"NEAR SPOTTSYLYANIA COURT HOUSE, VA.,
May 20, 1864.

"The enemy are evidently relying for supplies greatly on such as are brought over the branch road running through Staunton. On the whole, therefore, I think it would be better for General Hunter to move in that direction; reach Staunton and Gordonsville or Charlottesville, if he does not meet too much opposition. If he can hold at bay a force equal to his If he can hold at bay a force equal to his own, he will be doing good service.

"U.S. GRANT, Lieutenant General.

"Major General H.W. HALLECK."

"JERICHO FORD, VA., May 25, 1864.
"If Hunter can possibly get to Charlottesville and Lynchburg, he should do so, living on the country. The railroads and canal should be destroyed beyond possibility of repairs for weeks. Completing this, he could find his way back to his original base, or from about Gordonsville join this army.

"U.S. GRANT, Lieutenant General.

"Major General H.W. HALLECK."

General Hunter immediately took up the offensive, and moving up the Shenandoah Valley, met the enemy on the 5th of June at Piedmont, and after a battle of ten hours routed and defeated him, capturing on the field of battle 1,500 men, 3 pieces of artillery, and 300 stand of small-arms. On the 8th of the same month he formed a junction with Crook and Averill at Staunton, from which place he moved direct on Lynchburg, via Lexington, which place he reached and invested on the 16th day of June. Up to this time he was very successful, and but for the difficulty of taking with him sufficient ordnance stores over so long a march, through a hostile country, he would no doubt have captured that (to the enemy,) important point. The destruction of the enemy's supplies and manufactories was very great. To meet this movement under General Hunter, General Lee sent a force, perhaps equal to a corps, a part of which reached Lynchburg a short time before Hunter. After some skirmishing on the 17th and 18th, General Hunter, owing to a want of ammunition to give battle, retired from before the place. Unfortunately, this want of ammunition left him no choice of route for his return but by way of Kanawha. This lost to us the use of his troops for several weeks from the defence of the north.

Had General Hunter moved by way of Charlottesville, instead of Lexington, as his instructions contemplated, he would have been in a position to have covered the Shenandoah Valley against the enemy, should the force he met have seemed to endanger it. If it did not, he would have been within easy distance of the James river canal, on the main line of communication between Lynchburg and the force sent for its defence. I have never taken exception to the operations of General Hunter, and I am not now disposed to find fault with him, for I have no doubt he acted within what he conceived to be the spirit of his instructions and the interests of the service. The promptitude of his movements and his gallantry should entitle him to the commendation of his country. To return to the army of the Potomac: The 2d corps commenced crossing the James river on the morning of the 14th by ferry-boats at Wilcox's landing. The laying of the pontoon bridge was completed about midnight of the 14th, and the crossing of the remainder of the army was rapidly pushed forward by both bridge and ferry.

After the crossing had commenced, I proceeded by a steamer to Bermuda Hundred to give the necessary orders for the immediate capture of Petersburg.

The instruction to General Butler were verbal, and were for him to send General Smith immediately, that night, with all the troops he could give him without sacrificing the position he then held. I told him that I would return at once to the army of the Potomac, hasten its crossing, and throw it forward to Petersburg by divisions as rapidly as it could be done; that we could re-enforce our armies more rapidly there than the enemy could bring troops against us. General Smith got off as directed, and confronted the enemy's pickets near Petersburg before daylight next morning, but for some reason, that I have never been able to satisfactorily understand, did not get ready to assault his main lines until near sundown. Then, with a part of his command only, he made the assault, and carried the lines northeast of Petersburg from the Appomattox river, for a distance of over two and a half miles, capturing fifteen pieces of artillery and three hundred prisoners. This was about 7 P.M. Between the line thus captured and Petersburg there were no other works, and there was no evidence that the enemy had re-enforced Petersburg with a single brigade from any source. The night was clear – the moon shining brightly – and favorable to further operations. General Hancock, with two divisions of the 2d corps, reached General Smith just after dark, and offered the service of these troops as he (Smith) might wish, waiving rank to the named commander, who he naturally supposed knew best the position of affairs, and what to do with the troops. But instead of taking these troops, and pushing at once into Petersburg, he requested General Hancock to relieve a part of his line in the captured works, which was done before midnight.

By the time I arrived the next morning the enemy was in force. An attack was ordered to be made at 6 o'clock that evening by the troops under Smith and the 2d and 9th corps. It required until that time for the 9th corps to get up and into position. The attack was made as ordered, and the fighting continued with but little intermission until 6 o'clock the next morning, and resulted in our carrying the advance and some of the main works of the enemy to the right (our left) of those previously captured by General Smith, several pieces of artillery, and over four hundred prisoners.

The 5th corps having got up, the attacks were renewed and persisted in with great vigor on the 17th and 18th, but only resulted in forcing the enemy to an interior line from which he could not be dislodged. The advantages in position gained by us were very great. The army then proceeded to envelop Petersburg toward the Southside railroad, as far as possible, without attacking fortifications.

On the 6th the enemy, to re-enforce Petersburg, withdrew from a part of his entrenchment in front of Bermuda Hundred, expecting no doubt to get troops from north of the James to take the place of those withdrawn before we could discover it. General Butler, taking advantage of this, at once moved a force on the railroad between Petersburg and Richmond. As soon as I was apprised of the advantage thus gained, to retain it I ordered two divisions of the 6th corps, General Wright commanding, that were embarking at Wilcox's landing, under orders for City Point, to report to General Butler, at Bermuda Hundred of which General

Butler was notified, and the importance of holding a position in advance of his present line urged upon him.

About 2 o'clock in the afternoon General Butler was forced back to the line the enemy had withdrawn from in the morning. General Wright, with his two divisions, joined General Butler on the forenoon of the 17th, the latter still holding with a strong picket line the enemy's works. But instead of putting these divisions into the enemy's works to hold them, he permitted them to halt and rest some distance in the rear of his own line. Between 4 and 5 o'clock in the afternoon the enemy attacked and drove in his pickets and reoccupied his old line.

On the night of the 20th and morning of the 21st a lodgment was effected by General Butler, with one brigade of infantry, on the north bank of the James, at Deep Bottom, and connected the pontoon bridge with Bermuda Hundred.

On the 19th General Sheridan, on his return from his expedition against the Virginia Central railroad, arrived at the White House just as the enemy's cavalry was about to attack it, and compelled it to retire. The result of this expedition was, that General Sheridan met the enemy's cavalry near Trevillian Station on the morning of the 11th of June, whom he attacked, and after an obstinate contest drove from the field in complete rout. He left his dead and nearly all his wounded in our hands, and about four hundred prisoners and several hundred horses. On the 12th he destroyed the railroad from Trevillian Station to Louisa Court House. This occupied until 3 o'clock p.m., when he advanced in the direction of Gordonsville. He found the enemy re-enforced by infantry, behind well-constructed rifle-pits, about five miles from the latter place, and too strong to successfully assault. On the extreme right, however, his reserve brigade carried the enemy's works twice, and was twice driven there from by infantry. Night closed the contest. Not having sufficient ammunition to continue the engagement, and his animals being without forage, (the country furnishing but inferior grazing,) and hearing nothing from General Hunter, he withdrew his command to the north side of the North Anna, and commenced his return march, reaching White House at the time before stated. After breaking up the depot at that place he moved to the James river, which he reached safely after heavy fighting. He commenced crossing on the 25th, near Fort Powhatan, without further molestation, and rejoined the army of the Potomac.

On the 22d General Wilson, with his own division of cavalry of the army of the Potomac, and General Kautz's division of cavalry of the army of the James, moved against the enemy's railroads south of Richmond. Striking the Weldon railroad at Ream's Station, destroying the depot and several miles of the road and the Southside road about fifteen miles from Petersburg, to near Nottoway Station, where he met and defeated a force of the enemy's cavalry, he reached Burksville Station on the afternoon of the 23d, and from there destroyed the Danville railroad to Roanoke bridge, a distance of twenty-five miles, where he found the enemy in force, and in a position from which he could not dislodge him. He then commenced his return march, and on the 28th met the enemy's cavalry in force at the Weldon railroad crossing of Stony creek, where he had a severe but not decisive engagement. Thence he made a detour from his left, with a view of reaching Ream's Station, (supposing it to be in our possession.) At this place he was met by the enemy's cavalry, supported by infantry, and forced to retire, with the loss of his artillery and trains. In this last encounter General Kautz, with a part of his command, became separated, and made his way into our lines. General Wilson, with the remainder of his force, succeeded in crossing the Nottoway river and coming in safely on our left and rear. The damage to the enemy in this expedition more than compensated for the losses we sustained. It severed all connexion by railroad with Richmond for several weeks.

With a view of cutting the enemy's railroad from near Richmond to the Anna rivers and making him wary of the situation of his army in the Shenandoah, and, in the event of failure in this, to take advantage of his necessary withdrawal of troops from Petersburg, to explode a mine that had been prepared in front of the 9th corps and assault the enemy's lines at that place, on the night of the 26th of July the 2d corps and two divisions of the cavalry corps and Kautz's cavalry were crossed to the north bank of the James river and joined the force General Butler had there. On the 27th the enemy was driven from his intrenched position, with the loss of four pieces of artillery. On the 28th our lives were extended from Deep Bottom to New Market road, but in getting this position were attacked by the enemy in heavy force. The fighting lasted for several hours, resulting in considerable loss to both sides. The first object of this move having failed, by reason of the very large force thrown there by the enemy, I determined to take advantage of the diversion made, by assaulting Petersburg before he could get his force back there. One division of the 2d corps was withdrawn on the night of the 28th, and moved during the night to the rear of the 18th corps, to relieve that corps in the line, that it might be foot-loose in the assault to be made. The other two divisions of the 2d corps and Sheridan's cavalry were crossed over on the night of the 29th and moved in front of Petersburg. On the morning of the 30th, between four and five o'clock, the mine was sprung, blowing up a battery and most of a regiment, and the advance of the assaulting column, formed of the 9th corps, immediately took possession of the crater made by the explosion, and the line for some distance to the right and left of it, and a detached line in front of it, but for some cause failed to advance promptly to the ridge beyond. Had they done this, I have every reason to believe that Petersburg would have fallen. Other troops were immediately pushed forward, but the time consumed in getting them up enabled the enemy to rally from his surprise (which had been complete) and get forces to this point for its defence. The captured line thus held being untenable, and of no advantage to us, the troops were withdrawn, but not without heavy loss. Thus terminated in disaster what promised to be the most successful assault of the campaign.

Immediately upon the enemy's ascertaining that General Hunter was retreating from Lynchburg by way of the Kanawha river, thus laying the Shenandoah Valley open for raids into Maryland and Pennsylvania, he returned northward, and moved down that valley. As soon as this movement of the enemy was ascertained, General Hunter, who had reached the Kanawha river, was directed to move his troops without delay, by river and railroad, to Harper's Ferry; but owing to the difficulty of navigation by reason of low water and breaks in the railroad, great delay was experienced in getting there. It became necessary, therefore, to find other troops to check this movement of the enemy. For this purpose the 6th corps was taken from the armies operating against Richmond, to which was added the 19th corps, then fortunately beginning to arrive in Hampton roads from the Gulf department, under orders issued immediately after the ascertainment of the result of the Red river expedition. The garrisons of Baltimore and Washington were at this time made up of heavy artillery regiments, hundred-days men, and detachments from the invalid corps. One division under command of General Ricketts, of the 6th corps, was sent to Baltimore, and the remaining two divisions of the 6th corps, under General Wright, were subsequently sent to Washington. On the 3d of July the enemy approached Martinsburg; General Sigel, who was in command of our forces there, retreated across the Potomac at Shepardstown; and General Weber, commanding at Harper's Ferry, crossed the river and occupied Maryland heights. On the 6th the enemy occupied Hagerstown, moving a strong column towards Frederick city. General Wallace with Ricketts's division and his own command, the latter mostly new and undisciplined troops, pushed out from Baltimore with great promptness, and met the enemy in force on the Monocacy, near the crossing of the railroad bridge. His force was not sufficient to insure success, but he fought the enemy nevertheless, and although it resulted in a defeat to our arms, yet it detained the enemy and thereby served to enable General Wright to reach Washington with two divisions of the 6th corps, and the advance of the 19th corps, before him. From Monocacy the enemy moved on Washington, his cavalry advance reaching Rockville on the evening of the 10th. On the 12th a reconnoissance was thrown out in front of Fort Stevens, to ascertain the enemy's position and force. A severe skirmish ensued, in which we lost about 280 in killed and wounded. The enemy's loss was probably greater. He commenced retreating during the night. Learning the exact condition of affairs at Washington, I requested by telegraph, at 11:45 p.m. on the 12th, the assignment of Major General H. G. Wright to the command of all the troops that could be made available to operate in the field against the enemy, and directed that he should get outside of the trenches with all the force he could, and push Early to the last moment. General Wright commenced the pursuit on the 13th; on the 18th the enemy was overtaken at Snicker's ferry, on the Shenandoah, when a sharp skirmish occurred; and on the 20th General Averill encountered and defeated a portion of the rebel army at Winchester, capturing four pieces of artillery and several hundred prisoners.

Learning that Early was retreating south towards Lynchburg or Richmond, I directed that the 6th and 19th corps be got back to the armies operating against Richmond, so that they might be used in a movement against Lee before the return of the troops sent, by him into the valley; and that Hunter should remain in the Shenandoah valley, keeping between any force of the enemy and Washington, acting on the defensive as much as possible. I felt that if the enemy had any notion of returning, the fact would be developed before the 6th and 19th corps could leave Washington. Subsequently the 19th corps was excepted from the order to return to the James.

About the 25th it became evident that the enemy was again advancing upon Maryland and Pennsylvania, and the 6th corps, then at Washington, was ordered back to the vicinity of Harper's Ferry. The rebel force moved down the valley, and sent a raiding party into Pennsylvania, which on the 30th burned Chambersburg and then retreated, pursued by our cavalry, towards Cumberland. They were met and defeated by General Kelly, and with diminished numbers escaped into the mountains of West Virginia. From the time of the first raid the telegraph wires were frequently down between Washington and City Point, making it necessary to transmit messages a part of the way by boat. It took from twenty-four to thirty-six hours to get despatches through and return answers back; so that often orders would be given, and then information would be received showing a different state of facts from those on which they were based, causing a confusion and apparent contradiction of orders that must have considerably embarrassed those who had to execute them, and rendered operations against the enemy less effective than they otherwise would have been. To remedy this evil, it was evident to my mind that some person should have the supreme command of all the forces in the departments of West Virginia, Washington, Susquehanna and the middle department, and I so recommended.

On the 2d of August I ordered General Sheridan to report in person to Major General Halleck, chief of staff, at Washington, with a view to his assignment to the command of all the forces against Early. At this time the enemy was concentrated in the neighborhood of Winchester, whilst our forces, under General Hunter, were concentrated on the Monocacy, at the crossing of the Baltimore and Ohio railroad, leaving open to the enemy western Maryland and southern Pennsylvania. From where I was, I hesitated to give positive orders for the movement of our forces at Monocacy, lest by so doing I should expose Washington. Therefore, on the 4th I left City Point to visit Hunter's command, and determine for myself what was best to be done. On arrival there, and after consultation with General Hunter, I issued to him the following instructions:

"MONOCACY BRIDGE, MD.,
"August 5, 1864 – 8 p.m.

"GENERAL: Concentrate all your available force without delay in the vicinity of Harper's Ferry, leaving only such railroad guards and garrisons for public property as may be necessary. Use, in this concentrating, the railroads, if by so doing time can be saved.

From Harper's Ferry, if it is found that the enemy has moved north of the Potomac in large force, push north, following him and attacking him wherever found; follow him if driven south of the Potomac, as long as it is safe to do so. If it is ascertained that the enemy has but a small force north of the Potomac, then push south with the main force, detaching under a competent commander a sufficient force to look after the raiders, and drive them to their homes. In detaching such a force, the brigade of cavalry now en route from Washington via Rockville may be taken into account.

"There are now on their way to join you three other brigades of the best cavalry, numbering, at least, 5,000 men and horses. These will be instructed, in the absence of further orders, to join you by the south side of the Potomac. One brigade will probably start tomorrow. In pushing up the Shenandoah valley, where it is expected you will have to go east or last, it is desirable that nothing should be left to invite the enemy to return. Take all provisions, forage, and stock wanted for the use of your command; such as cannot be consumed, destroy. It is not desirable that the buildings should be destroyed – they should rather be protected – but the people should be informed that so long as an army can subsist among them recurrences of these raids must be expected, and we are determined to stop them at all hazards.

"Bear in mind the object is to drive the enemy south, and to do this you want to keep him always in sight. Be guided in your course by the course he takes. "Make your own arrangements for supplies of all kinds, giving regular vouchers for such as may be taken from loyal citizens in the country through which you march.

"U. S. GRANT, Lieutenant General.

"Major General D. HUNTER."

The troops were immediately put in motion, and the advance reached Halltown that night.

General Hunter having, in our conversation, expressed a willingness to be relieved from command, I telegraphed to have General Sheridan, then at Washington, sent to Harper's Ferry by the morning train, with orders to take general command of all the troops in the field, and to call on General Hunter at Monocacy, who would turn over to him my letter of instructions. I remained at Monocacy, until General Sheridan arrived, on the morning of the 6th, and, after a conference with him in relation to military affairs in that vicinity, I returned to City Point by way of Washington.

On the 7th of August the middle department and the departments of West Virginia, Washington, and Susquehanna were constituted into the "Middle military division," and Major General Sheridan was assigned to temporary command of the same.

Two divisions of cavalry, commanded by Generals Torbert and Wilson, were sent to Sheridan from the army of the Potomac. The first reached him at Harper's Ferry about the 11th of August.

His operations during the month of August and the fore part of September were both of an offensive and defensive character, resulting in many severe skirmishes, principally by the cavalry, in which we were generally successful, but no general engagement took place. The two armies lay in such a position – the enemy on the west bank of the Opequan creek covering Winchester, and our forces in front of Berrysville – that either could bring on a battle at any time. Defeat to us would lay open to the enemy the States of Maryland and Pennsylvania for long distances before another army could be interposed to check him. Under these circumstances, I hesitated about allowing the initiative to be taken. Finally, the use of the Baltimore and Ohio railroad and the Chesapeake and Ohio canal, which were both obstructed by the enemy, became so indispensably necessary to us, and the importance of relieving Pennsylvania and Maryland from continuously threatened invasion so great, that I determined the risk should be taken. But fearing to telegraph the order for an attack without knowing more than I did of General Sheridan's feelings as to what would be the probable result, I left City Point on the 15th of September to visit him at his headquarters, to decide, after conference with him, what should be done. I met him at Charleston, and he pointed out so distinctly how each army lay; what he could do the moment he was authorized, and expressed such confidence of success, that I saw there were but two words of instructions necessary – Go in! For the convenience of forage, the teams for supplying the army were kept at Harper's Ferry. I asked him if he could get out his teams and supplies in time to make an attack on the ensuing Tuesday morning. His reply was, that he could before daylight on Monday. He was oft promptly to time, and I may here add that the result was such that I have never since deemed it necessary to visit General Sheridan before giving him orders.

Early on the morning of the 19th General Sheridan attacked General Early at the crossing on the Opequan creek, and after a most sanguinary and bloody battle, lasting until 5 o'clock in the evening, defeated; him with heavy loss, carrying his entire position from Opequan creek to Winchester, capturing several thousand prisoners and five pieces of artillery. The enemy rallied and made a stand in a strong position at Fisher's Hill, where he was attacked and again defeated with heavy loss on the 20th. Sheridan pursued him with great energy through Harrisonburg, Staunton, and the gaps of the Blue Ridge. After stripping the upper valley of most of the supplies and provisions for the rebel army, he returned to Strasburg, and took position on the north side of Cedar creek.

Having received considerable re-enforcements, General Early again returned to the valley, and on the 9th of October his cavalry encountered ours near Strasburg, where the rebels were defeated with the loss of eleven pieces of artillery and 350 prisoners. On the night of the 18th the enemy crossed the mountains which separated the branches of the Shenandoah, forded the north fork, and early on the morning of the 19th, under cover of the darkness and the fog, surprised and turned our left flank, and captured the batteries which enfiladed our whole line. Our troops fell back with heavy loss and in much confusion, but were finally rallied between Middletown and Newtown. At this juncture General Sheridan, who was at Winchester when the battle commenced, arrived on the field, arranged his lines just in time to repulse a heavy attack of the enemy, and immediately assuming the offensive, he attacked in turn with great vigor. The enemy was defeated with great slaughter and the loss of most of his artillery and trains and the trophies he had captured in the morning. The wreck of his army escaped during the night, and fled in the direction of Staunton and Lynchburg. Pursuit was made to Mount Jackson. Thus ended this, the enemy's last attempt to invade the north via the Shenandoah Valley. I was now enabled to return the 6th corps to the army of the Potomac, and to send one division from Sheridan's army to the army of the James, and another to Savannah, Georgia, to hold Sherman's new acquisitions on the sea-coast, and thus enable him to move without detaching from his force for that purpose.

Reports from various sources led me to believe that the enemy had detached three divisions from Petersburg to re-enforce Early in the Shenandoah Valley. I therefore sent the 2d corps and Gregg's division of cavalry, of the army of the Potomac, and a force of General Butler's army, on the night of the 13th of August, to threaten Richmond from the north side of the James, to prevent him from sending troops away, and, if possible, to draw back those sent. In this move we captured six pieces of artillery and several hundred prisoners, detained troops that were under marching orders, and ascertained that but one division, (Kershaw's) of the three reputed detached, had gone.

The enemy having withdrawn heavily from Petersburg to resist this movement, the 5th corps, General Warren commanding, was moved out on the 18th and took possession of the Weldon railroad. During the day he had considerable fighting. To regain possession of the road, the enemy made repeated and desperate assaults, but was each time repulsed with great loss. On the night of the 20th the troops on the north side of the James were withdrawn, and Hancock and Gregg returned to the front of Petersburg. On the 25th the 2d Corps and Gregg's division of cavalry, while at Ream's Station destroying the railroad, were attacked, and after desperate fighting, a part of our line gave way, and five pieces of artillery fell into the hands of the enemy.

By the 12th of September a branch railroad was completed from the City Point and Petersburg railroad to the Weldon railroad, enabling us to supply, without difficulty, in all weather, the army in front of Petersburg.

The extension of our lines across the Weldon railroad compelled the enemy to so extend his that it seemed he could have but few troops north of the James for the defence of Richmond. On the night of the 28th the 10th corps, Major General Birney, and the 18th corps, Major General Ord commanding, of General Butler's army, were crossed to the north side of the James, and advanced on the morning of the 29th, carrying the very strong fortifications and intrenchments below Chapin's farm, known as Fort Harrison, capturing fifteen pieces of artillery and the New Market road and intrenchments. This success was followed up by a gallant assault upon Fort Gillmore, immediately in front of the Chapin farm fortifications, in which we were repulsed with heavy loss. Kautz's cavalry was pushed forward on the road to the right of this, supported by infantry, and reached the enemy's inner line, but was unable to get further. The position captured from the enemy was so threatening to Richmond that I determined to hold it. The enemy made several desperate attempts to dislodge us, all of which were unsuccessful, and for which he paid dearly. On the morning of the 30th General Meade sent out a reconnaissance, with a view to attacking the enemy's line if it was found sufficiently weakened by withdrawal of troops to the north side. In this reconnaissance we captured and held the enemy's works near Poplar Spring church. In the afternoon troops moving to get to the left of the point gained were attacked by the enemy in heavy force, and compelled to fall back until supported by the forces holding the captured works. Our cavalry under Gregg was also attacked, but repulsed the enemy with great loss.

On the 7th of October the enemy attacked Kautz's cavalry north of the James, and drove it back with heavy loss in killed, wounded and prisoners, and the loss of all the artillery – eight or nine pieces. This he followed up by an attack on our intrenched infantry line, but was repulsed with severe slaughter. On the 13th a reconnaissance was sent out by General Butler, with a view to drive the enemy from some new works he was constructing, which resulted in very heavy loss to us.

On the 27th the army of the Potomac, leaving only sufficient men to hold its fortified line, moved by the enemy's right flank. The 2d corps, followed by two divisions of the 5th corps, with the cavalry in advance and covering our left flank, forced a passage of Hatcher's run, and moved up the south side of it towards the South Side railroad, until the 2d corps and part of the cavalry reached the Boydton plank road, where it crosses Hatcher's run. At this point we were six miles distant from the South Side railroad, which I had hoped by this movement to reach and hold. But finding that we had not reached the end of the enemy's fortifications, and no place presenting itself for a successful assault by which he might be doubled up and shortened, I determined to withdraw to within our fortified line. Orders were given accordingly. Immediately upon receiving a report that General Warren had connected with General Hancock, I returned to my headquarters. Soon after I left, the enemy moved out across Hatcher's run, in the gap between Generals Hancock and Warren, which was not closed as reported, and made a desperate attack on General Hancock's right and rear. General Hancock immediately faced his corps to meet it, and after a bloody combat drove the enemy within his works, and withdrew that night to his old position.

In support of this movement General Butler made a demonstration on the north side of the James, and attacked the enemy on the Williamsburg road, and also on the York river railroad. In the former he was unsuccessful; in the latter he succeeded in carrying a work which was afterwards abandoned, and his forces withdrawn to their former positions.

From this time forward the operations in front of Petersburg and Richmond, until the spring campaign of 1865, were confined to the defence and extension of our lines, and to offensive movements for crippling the enemy's lines of communication, and to prevent his detaching any considerable force to send south. By the 7th of February our lines were extended to Hatcher's run, and the Weldon railroad had been destroyed to Hicksford.

General Sherman moved from Chattanooga on the 6th of May, with the armies of the Cumberland, Tennessee, and Ohio, commanded, respectively, by Generals Thomas, McPherson, and Schofield, upon Johnston's army at Dalton; but finding the enemy's positions at Buzzard Roost, covering Dalton, too strong to be assaulted, General McPherson was sent through Snake Gap to turn it, whilst Generals Thomas and Schofield threatened it in front and on the north. This movement was successful. Johnston, finding his retreat likely to be cut off, fell back to his fortified position at Resaca, where he was attacked on the afternoon of May 15th. A heavy battle ensued. During the night the enemy retreated south. Late on the 17th his rear guard was overtaken near Adairsville, and heavy skirmishing followed. The next morning, however, he had again disappeared. He was vigorously pursued and was overtaken at Cassville on the 19th, but, during the ensuing night, retreated across the Etowah. Whilst these operations were going on, General Jefferson C. Davis's division of Thomas's army was sent to Rome, capturing it with its forts and artillery and its valuable mills and foundries. General Sherman having given his army a few days' rest at this point, again put it in motion on the 23d for Dallas, with a view of turning the difficult pass at Allatoona. On the afternoon of the 25th the advance, under General Hooker, had a severe battle with the enemy, driving him back to New Hope church, near Dallas.

Several sharp encounters occurred at this point. The most important was on the 28th, when the enemy assaulted General McPherson at Dallas, but received a terrible and bloody repulse.

On the 4th of June Johnston abandoned his intrenched position at New Hope church and retreated to the strong positions of Kenesaw, Pine, and Lost mountains. He was forced to yield the two last named places and concentrate his army on Kenesaw, where, on the 27th, Generals Thomas and McPherson made a determined but unsuccessful assault. On the night of the 2d of July Sherman commenced moving his army by the right flank, and on the morning of the 3d found that the enemy, in consequence of this movement, had abandoned Kenesaw and retreated across the Chattahoochie.

General Sherman remained on the Chattahoochie to give his men rest and get up stores until the 17th of July, when he resumed his operations, crossed the Chattahoochie, destroyed a large portion of the railroad to Augusta, and drove the enemy back to Atlanta. At this place General Hood succeeded General Johnston in command of the rebel army, and assuming the offensive-defensive policy, made several severe attacks upon Sherman in the vicinity of Atlanta, the most desperate and determined of which was on the 22d of July. About 1 p.m. of this day the brave, accomplished, and noble-hearted McPherson was killed. General Logan succeeded him, and commanded the army of the Tennessee through this desperate battle, and until he was superseded by Major General Howard, on the 26th, with the same success and ability that had characterized him in the command of a corps or division.

In all these attacks the enemy was repulsed with great loss. Finding it impossible to entirely invest the place, General Sherman, after securing his line of communications across the Chattahoochie, moved his main force round by the enemy's left flank upon the Montgomery and Macon roads, to draw the enemy from his fortifications. In this he succeeded, and, after defeating the enemy near Rough and Ready, Jonesboro', and Lovejoy's, forcing him to retreat to the south, on the 2d of September occupied Atlanta, the objective point of his campaign.

About the time of this move the rebel cavalry, under Wheeler, attempted to cut his communications in the rear, but was repulsed at Dalton and driven into East Tennessee, whence it proceeded west to McMinnville, Murfreesboro', and Franklin, and was finally driven south of the Tennessee. The damage done by this raid was repaired in a few days.

During the partial investment of Atlanta, General Rousseau joined General Sherman with a force of cavalry from Decatur, having made a successful raid upon the Atlanta and Montgomery railroad, and its branches near Opelika. Cavalry raids were also made by Generals McCook, Garrard and Stoneman to cut the remaining railroad communication with Atlanta. The first two were successful – the latter disastrous.

General Sherman's movement from Chattanooga to Atlanta was prompt, skilful and brilliant. The history of his flank movements and battles during that memorable campaign will ever be read with an interest unsurpassed by anything in history.

His own report, and those of his subordinate commanders accompanying it, give the details of that most successful campaign.

He was dependent for the supply of his armies upon a single-track railroad from Nashville to the point where he was operating. This passed the entire distance through a hostile country, and every foot of it had to be protected by troops. The cavalry force of the enemy under Forrest, in northern Mississippi, was evidently waiting for Sherman to advance far enough into the mountains of Georgia to make a retreat disastrous, to get upon his line and destroy it beyond the possibility of further use. To guard against this danger Sherman left what he supposed to be a sufficient force to operate against Forrest in West Tennessee. He directed General Washburn, who commanded there, to send Brigadier General S. D. Sturgis in command of this force to attack him. On the morning of the 10th of June General Sturgis met the enemy near Guntown, Mississippi, was badly beaten, and driven back in utter rout and confusion to Memphis, a distance of about one hundred miles, hotly pursued by the enemy. By this, however, the enemy was defeated in his designs upon Sherman's line of communications. The persistency with which he followed up this success exhausted him, and made a season for rest and repairs necessary. In the mean time Major General A. J. Smith, with the troops of the army of the Tennessee that had been sent by General Sherman to General Banks, arrived at Memphis on their return from Red river, where they had done most excellent service. He was directed by General Sherman to immediately take the offensive against Forrest. This he did with the promptness and effect which has characterized his whole military career. On the 14th of July he met the enemy at Tupelo, Mississippi, and whipped him badly. The fighting continued through three days. Our loss was small compared with that of the enemy. Having accomplished the object of his expedition, General Smith returned to Memphis.

During the months of March and April this same force under Forrest annoyed us considerably. On the 24th of March it captured Union City, Kentucky, and its garrison, and on the 24th attacked Paducah, commanded by Colonel S.G. Hicks, 40th Illinois volunteers. Colonel H., having but a small force, withdrew to the forts near the river, from where he repulsed the enemy and drove him from the place.

On the 13th of April, part of this force, under the rebel General Buford, summoned the garrison of Columbus, Kentucky, to surrender, but received for reply from Colonel Lawrence, 34th New Jersey volunteers, that, being placed there by his government with adequate force to hold his post and repel all enemies from it, surrender was out of the question.

On the morning of the same day Forrest attacked Fort Pillow, Tennessee, garrisoned by a detachment of Tennessee cavalry, and the 1st regiment Alabama colored troops, commanded by Major Booth. The garrison fought bravely until about 3 o'clock in the afternoon, when the enemy carried the works by assault; and, after our men threw down their arms, proceeded to an inhuman and merciless massacre of the garrison.

On the 14th, General Buford, having failed at Columbus, appeared before Paducah, but was again driven off.

Guerillas and raiders, seemingly emboldened by Forrest's operations, were also very active in Kentucky. The most noted of these was Morgan. With a force of from two to three thousand cavalry he entered the State through Pound Gap in the latter part of May. On the 11th of June he attacked and captured Cynthiana, with its entire garrison. On the 12th he was overtaken by General Burbridge, and completely routed with heavy loss, and was finally driven out of the State. This notorious guerilla was afterwards surprised and killed near Greenville, Tennessee, and his command captured and dispersed by General Gillem.

In the absence of official reports at the commencement of the Red river expedition, except so far as relates to the movements of the troops sent by General Sherman under A. J. Smith, I am unable to give the date of its starting. The troops under General Smith, comprising two divisions of the 16th and a detachment of the 17th army corps, left Vicksburg on the 10th of March and reached the designated point on Red river one day earlier than that appointed by General Banks. The rebel forces at Fort De Russey, thinking to defeat him, left the fort on the 14th to give him battle in the open field; but, while occupying the enemy with skirmishing and demonstrations, Smith pushed forward to Fort De Russey, which had been left with a weak garrison, and captured it with its garrison – about 350 men, 11 pieces of artillery, and many small-arms. Our loss was but slight. On the 15th he pushed forward to Alexandria, which place he reached on the 18th. On the 21st he had an engagement with the enemy at Henderson Hill, in which he defeated him, capturing 210 prisoners and 4 pieces of artillery.

On the 28th he again attacked and defeated the enemy under the rebel General Taylor at Cane river. By the 26th General Banks had assembled his whole army at Alexandria and pushed forward to Grand Ecore. On the morning of April 6 he moved from Grand Ecore. On the afternoon of the 7th his advance engaged the enemy near Pleasant Hill and drove him from the field. On the same afternoon the enemy made a stand eight miles beyond Pleasant Hill, but was again compelled to retreat. On the 8th, at Sabine Cross-roads and Peach Hill, the enemy attacked and defeated his advance, capturing nineteen pieces of artillery and an immense amount of transportation and stores. During the night General Banks fell back to Pleasant Hill, where another battle was fought on the 9th, and the enemy repulsed with great loss. During the night General Banks continued his retrograde movement to Grand Ecore, and thence to Alexandria, which he reached on the 27th of April. Here a serious difficulty arose in getting Admiral Porter's fleet, which accompanied the expedition, over the rapids, the water having fallen so much since they passed up as to prevent their return. At the suggestion of Colonel (now Brigadier General) Bailey, and under his superintendence, wing-dams were constructed, by which the channel was contracted so that the fleet passed down the rapids in safety.

The army evacuated Alexandria on the 14th of May, after considerable skirmishing with the enemy's advance, and reached Morganzia and Point Coupée near the end of the month. The disastrous termination of this expedition, and the lateness of the season rendered impracticable the carrying out of my plans of a movement in force sufficient to insure the capture of Mobile.

On the 23d of March Major General Steele left Little Rock with the 7th army corps to co-operate with General Banks's expedition on Red river, and reached Arkadelphia on the 28th. On the 16th of April, after driving the enemy before him, he was joined near Elkin's ferry, in Washita county, by General Thayer, who had marched from Fort Smith. After several severe skirmishes, in which the enemy was defeated, General Steele reached Camden, which he occupied about the middle of April.

On learning the defeat and consequent retreat of General Banks on Red river, and the loss of one of his own trains at Mark's mill, in Dallas County, General Steele determined to fall back to the Arkansas river. He left Camden on the 26th of April, and reached Little Rock on the 2d of May. On the 30th of April the enemy attacked him while crossing Saline river at Jenkins's ferry, but was repulsed with considerable loss. Our loss was about 600 in killed, wounded, and prisoners.

Major General Canby, who had been assigned to the command of the "military division of west Mississippi," was therefore directed to send the 19th army corps to join the armies operating against Richmond, and to limit the remainder of his command to such operations as might be necessary to hold the positions and lines of communications he then occupied.

Before starting General A. J. Smith's troops back to Sherman, General Canby sent a part of it to disperse a force of the enemy that was collecting near the Mississippi river. General Smith met and defeated this force near Lake Chicot on the 5th of June. Our loss was about 40 killed and 70 wounded.

In the latter part of July General Canby sent Major General Gordon Granger, with such forces as he could collect, to co-operate with Admiral Farragut against the defences of Mobile bay. On the 8th of August Fort Gaines surrendered to the combined naval and land forces. Fort Powell was blown up and abandoned.

On the 9th Fort Morgan was invested, and after a severe bombardment surrendered on the 23d. The total captures amounted to 1,464 prisoners and 104 pieces of artillery.

About the last of August, it being reported that the rebel General Price, with a force of about 10,000 men, had reached Jacksonport, on his way to invade Missouri, General A. J. Smith's command, then en route from Memphis to join Sherman, was ordered to Missouri. A cavalry force was also, at the same time, sent from Memphis, under command of Colonel Winslow. This made General Rosecrans's forces superior to those of Price, and no doubt was entertained he would be able to check Price and drive him back, while the forces under General Steele, in Arkansas, would cut off his retreat. On the 26th day of September Price attacked Pilot Knob and forced the garrison to retreat, and thence moved north to the Missouri river, and continued up that river towards Kansas. General Curtis, commanding department of

Kansas, immediately collected such forces as he could to repel the invasion of Kansas, while General Rosecrans's cavalry was operating in his rear.

The enemy was brought to battle on the Big Blue and defeated, with the loss of nearly all his artillery and trains and a large number of prisoners. He made a precipitate retreat to northern Arkansas. The impunity with which Price was enabled to roam over the State of Missouri for a long time, and the incalculable mischief done by him, shows to how little purpose a superior force may be used. There is no reason why General Rosecrans should not have concentrated his forces and beaten and driven Price before the latter reached Pilot Knob.

September 20 the enemy's cavalry, under Forrest, crossed the Tennessee near Waterloo, Alabama, and on the 23d attacked the garrison at Athens, consisting of six hundred men, which capitulated on the 24th. Soon after the points he might be expected to move on this side of Charlotte, North Carolina. In answer the following telegram was sent him:

"CITY POINT, VA., February 25, 1865.

"GENERAL: Sherman's movements will depend on the amount of opposition he meets with from the enemy. If strongly opposed, he may possibly have to fall back to Georgetown, S. C., and fit out for a new start. I think, however, all danger for the necessity of going to that point has passed. I believe he has passed Charlotte. He may take Fayetteville on his way to Goldsboro'. If you reach Lynchburg, you will have to be guided in your after movements by the information you obtain. Before you could possibly reach Sherman, I think you would find him moving from

Goldsboro' towards Raleigh, or engaging the enemy strongly posted at one or the other of these places, with railroad communications opened from his army to Wilmington or Newbern.

"U. S. GRANT, Lieutenant General.

"Major General P. H. SHERIDAN."

General Sheridan moved from Winchester on the 27th of February, with two divisions of cavalry, numbering about 5,000 each. On the 1st of March he secured the bridge, which the enemy attempted to destroy, across the middle fork of the Shenandoah, at Mount Crawford, and entered Staunton on the 2d, the enemy having retreated on Waynesboro'. Thence he pushed on to Waynesboro', where he found the enemy in force in an intrenched position, under General Early. Without stopping to make a reconnaissance, an immediate attack was made, the position was carried, and 1,600 prisoners, 11 pieces of artillery, with horses and caissons complete, 200 wagons and teams loaded with subsistence, and 17 battle flags, were captured. The prisoners, under an escort of 1,500 men, were sent back to Winchester. Thence he marched on Charlottesville, destroying effectually the railroad and bridges as he went, which place he reached on the 3d. Here he remained two days, destroying the railroad toward Richmond and Lynchburg, including the large iron bridges over the north and south forks of the Rivanna river, and awaiting the arrival of his trains. This necessary delay caused him to abandon the idea of capturing Lynchburg. On the morning of the 6th, dividing his force into two columns, he sent one to Scottsville, whence it marched up the James river canal to New Market, destroying every lock, and in many places the bank of the canal. From here a force was pushed out from this column to Duiguidsville, to obtain possession of the bridge across the James river at that place, but failed. The enemy burned it on our approach. The enemy also burned the bridge across the river at Hardwicksville. The other column moved down the railroad toward Lynchburg, destroying it as far as Amherst Court-House, sixteen miles from Lynchburg; thence across the country, uniting with the column at New Market. The river being very high, his pontoons would not reach across it; and the enemy having destroyed the bridges by which he had hoped to cross the river and get on the South Side railroad about Farmville, and destroy it to Appomattox Court-House, the only thing left for him was to return to Winchester or strike a base at the White House. Fortunately, he chose the latter. From New Market he took up his line of march, following the canal towards Richmond, destroying every lock upon it and cutting the banks wherever practicable, to a point eight miles east of Goochland, concentrating the whole force at Columbia on the 10th. Here he rested one day, and sent through by scouts information of his whereabouts and purposes, and a request for supplies to meet him at White House, which reached me on the night of the 12th. An infantry force was immediately sent to get possession of White House, and supplies were forwarded. Moving from Columbia in a direction to threaten Richmond, to near Ashland Station, he crossed the Annas, and after having destroyed all the bridges and many miles of the railroad, proceeded down the north bank of the Pamunky to White House, which place he reached on the 19th.

Previous to this the following communication was sent to General Thomas:

Report of

"CITY POINT, VA., March 7, 1865 – 9:30 a.m.

"GENERAL: I think it will be advisable now for you to repair the railroad in East Tennessee, and throw a good force up to Bull's Gap and fortify there. Supplies at Knoxville could always be got forward as required. With Bull's Gap fortified, you can occupy as outposts about all of East Tennessee, and be prepared, if it should be required of you in the spring, to make a campaign towards Lynchburg, or into North Carolina. I do not think Stoneman should break the road until he gets into Virginia, unless it should be to cut off rolling stock that may be caught west of that.

"U. S. GRANT, Lieutenant General.

"Major General G. H. THOMAS."

Thus it will be seen that in March, 1865 General Canby was moving an adequate force against Mobile and the, army defending it under General Dick Taylor; Thomas was pushing out two large and well-appointed cavalry expeditions – one from Middle Tennessee under Brevet Major General Wilson against the enemy's vital points in Alabama, the other from East Tennessee under Major General Stoneman towards Lynchburg – and assembling the remainder of his available forces, preparatory to offensive operations from East Tennessee; General Sheridan's cavalry was at White House; the armies of the Potomac and James were confronting the enemy under Lee in his defences of Richmond and Petersburg; General Sherman with his armies, re-enforced by that of General Schofield, was at Goldsboro'; General Pope was making preparations for a spring campaign against the enemy under Kirby Smith and Price, west of the

Mississippi; and General Hancock was concentrating a force in the vicinity of Winchester, Virginia, to guard against invasion or to operate offensively, as might prove necessary.

After the long march by General Sheridan's cavalry over winter roads, it was necessary to rest and refit at White House. At this time the greatest source of uneasiness to me was the fear that the enemy would leave his strong lines about Petersburg and Richmond for the purpose of uniting with Johnston, before he was driven from them by battle, or I was prepared to make an effectual pursuit. On the 24th of March General Sheridan moved from White House, crossed the James River at Jones's landing, and formed a junction with the army of the Potomac in front of Petersburg on the 27th. During this move General Ord sent forces to cover the crossings of the Chickahominy.

On the 24th of March the following instructions for a general movement of the armies operating against Richmond were issued:

"CITY POINT, VA., March 24, 1865.

"GENERAL: On the 29th instant the armies operating against Richmond will be moved by our left for the double purpose of turning the enemy out of his present position around Petersburg; and to insure the success of the cavalry under General Sheridan, which will start at the same time, in its efforts to reach and destroy the South Side and Danville railroads. Two corps of the army of the Potomac will be moved at first in two columns, taking the two roads crossing Hatcher's run nearest where the present line held by us strikes that stream, both moving towards Dinwiddie Court-House.

"The cavalry under General Sheridan, joined by the division now under General Davies, will move at the same time by the Weldon road and the Jerusalem plank road, turning west from the latter before crossing the Nottoway, and west with the whole column before reaching Stony creek. General Sheridan will then move independently, under other instructions which will be given him. All dismounted cavalry belonging to the army of the Potomac, and the dismounted cavalry from the middle military division not required for guarding property belonging to their arm of service, will report to Brigadier General Benham, to be added to the defences of City Point. Major General Parke will be left in command of all the army left for holding the lines about Petersburg and City Point, subject, of course, to orders from the commander of the army of the Potomac. The 9th army corps will be left intact to hold the present line of works so long as the whole line now occupied by us is held. If, however, the troops to the left of the 9th corps are withdrawn, then the left of the corps may be thrown back so as to occupy the position held by the army prior to the capture of the Weldon road. All troops to the left of the 9th corps will be held in readiness to move at the shortest notice by such route as may be designated when the order is given.

"General Ord will detach three divisions, two white and one colored, or so much of them as he can, and hold his present lines, and march for the present left of the army of the Potomac. In the absence of further orders, or until further orders are given, the white divisions will follow the left column of the army of the Potomac, and the colored division the right column. During the movement Major General Weitzel will be left in command of all the forces remaining behind from the army of the James.

"The movement of troops from the army of the James will commence on the night of the 27th instant. General Ord will leave behind the minimum number of cavalry necessary for picket duty, in the absence of the main army. A cavalry expedition from General Ord's command will also be started from Suffolk, to leave there on Saturday, the 1st of April, under Colonel Sumner, for the purpose of cutting the railroad about Hicksford. This, if accomplished, will have to be a surprise, and therefore from three to five hundred men will be sufficient. They should, however, be supported by all the infantry that can be spared from Norfolk and Portsmouth, as far out as to where the cavalry crosses the Blackwater. The crossing should probably be at Uniten. Should Colonel Sumner succeed in reaching the Weldon road he will be instructed to do all the damage possible to the triangle of roads between Hicksford, Weldon, and Gaston. The railroad bridge at Weldon being fitted up for the passage of carriages, it might be practicable to destroy any accumulation of supplies the enemy may have collected south of the Roanoke. All the troops will move with four days rations in haversacks, and eight days' in wagons. To avoid as much hauling as possible, and to give the army of the James the same number of days' supply with the army of the Potamac, General Bird will direct his commissary and quartermaster to have sufficient supplies delivered at the terminus of the road to fill up in passing. Sixty rounds of ammunition per man will be taken in wagons, and as much grain as the transportation on hand will carry, after taking the specified amount of other supplies. The densely wooded country in which the army has to operate making the use of much artillery impracticable, the amount taken with the army will be reduced to six or eight guns to each division, at the option of the army commanders.

"All necessary preparations for carrying these directions into operation may be commenced at once. The reserves of the 9th corps should be massed as much as possible. Whilst I would not now order an unconditional attack on the enemy's line by them, they should be ready, and should make the attack if the enemy weakens his line in their front, without waiting for orders. In case they carry the line, then the whole of the 9th corps could follow up so as to join or co-operate with the balance of the army. To prepare for this, the 9th corps will have rations issued to them, same as the balance of the army. General Weitzel will keep vigilant watch upon his front, and if found at all practicable to break through at any point, he will do so. A success north of the James should be followed up with great promptness. An attack will not be feasible unless it is found that the enemy has detached largely. In that case it may be regarded as evident that the enemy are relying upon their local reserves, principally, for the defence of Richmond. Preparations may be made for abandoning all the lines north of the James, except enclosed works – only to be abandoned, however, after a break is made in the lines of the enemy.

"By these instructions a large part of the armies operating against Richmond is left behind. The enemy, knowing this, may, as an only chance, strip their lines to the merest skeleton, in the hope of advantage not being taken of it, whilst they hurl everything against the moving column, and return. It cannot be impressed too strongly upon commanders of troops left in the trenches not to allow this to occur without taking advantage of it. The very fact of the enemy coming out to attack, if he does so, might be regarded as almost conclusive evidence of such a weakening of his lines. I would have it particularly enjoined upon corps commanders that, in case of an attack from the enemy, those not attacked are not to wait for orders from the commanding officer of the army to which they belong, but that they will move promptly, and notify the commander of their action. I would also enjoin the same action on the part of division commanders when other parts of their corps are engaged. In like manner, I would urge the importance of following up a repulse of the enemy.

"U. S. GRANT, Lieutenant General.

"Major Generals MEADE, ORD, and SHERIDAN."

Early on the morning of the 25th the enemy assaulted our lines in front of the 9th corps (which held from the Appomattox river towards our left) and carried Fort Steadman, and a part of the line to the right and left of it, established themselves and turned the guns of the fort against us; but our troops on either flank held their ground until the reserves were brought up, when the enemy was driven back with a heavy loss in killed and wounded and 1,900 prisoners. Our loss was 68 killed, 337 wounded, and 506 missing. General Meade at once ordered the other corps to advance and feel the enemy in their respective fronts. Pushing forward, they captured and held the enemy's strongly intrenched picket line in front of the 2d and 6th corps, and 834 prisoners. The enemy made desperate attempts to retake this line, but without success. Our loss in front of these was 52 killed, 864 wounded, and 297 missing. The enemy's loss in killed and wounded was far greater.

General Sherman having got his troops all quietly in camp about Goldsboro', and his preparations for furnishing supplies to them perfected, visited me at City Point on the 27th of March, and stated that he would be ready to move, as he had previously written me, by the 10th of April, fully equipped and rationed for twenty days, if it should become necessary to bring his command to bear against Lee's army, in co-operation with our forces in front of Richmond and Petersburg. General Sherman proposed in this movement to threaten Raleigh, and then, by turning suddenly to the right, reach the Roanoke at Gaston or thereabouts, whence he could move on to the Richmond and Danville railroad, striking it in the vicinity of Burkesville, or join the armies operating against Richmond, as might be deemed best. This plan he was directed to carry into execution, if he received no further directions in the mean time. I explained to him the movement I had ordered to commence on the 29th of March. That if it should not prove as entirely successful as I hoped, I would cut the cavalry loose to destroy the Danville and South Side railroads, and thus deprive the enemy of further supplies, and also prevent the rapid concentration of Lee's and Johnston's armies.

I had spent days of anxiety lest each morning should bring the report that the enemy had retreated the night before. I was firmly convinced that Sherman's crossing the Roanoke would be the signal for Lee to leave. With Johnston and him combined, a long, tedious, and expensive campaign, consuming most of the summer, might become necessary. By moving out I would put the army in better condition for pursuit, and would at least, by the destruction of the Danville road, retard the concentration of the two armies of Lee and Johnston, and cause the enemy to abandon much material that he might otherwise save. I therefore determined not to delay the movement ordered.

On the night of the 27th Major General Ord, with two divisions of the 24th corps, Major General Gibbon commanding, and one division of the 25th corps, Brigadier General Birney commanding, and McKenzie's cavalry, took up his line of march in pursuance of the foregoing instructions, and reached the position assigned him near Hatcher's run on the morning of the 29th. On the 28th the following instructions were given to General Sheridan:

"CITY POINT, VA., March 28, 1865.

"GENERAL: The 5th army corps will move by the Vaughn road at 3 a.m. tomorrow morning. The 2d moves at about 9 a.m., having but about three miles to march to reach the point designated for it to take on the right of the 5th corps, after the latter reaching Dinwiddie Court House. Move your cavalry at as early an hour as you can, and without being confined to any particular road or roads. You may go out by the nearest roads in rear of the 5th corps, pass by its left, and, passing near to or through Dinwiddie, reach the right and rear of the enemy as soon as you can. It is not the intention to attack the enemy in his intrenched position, but to force him out, if possible. Should he come out and attack us, or get himself where he can be attacked, move in with your entire force in your own way, and with the full reliance that the army will engage or follow, as circumstances will dictate. I shall be on the field, and will probably be able to communicate with you. Should I not do so, and you find that the enemy keeps within his main intrenched line, you may cut loose and push for the Danville road. If you find it practicable, I would like you to cross the South Side road, between Petersburg and Burkesville, and destroy it to some extent. I would not advise much detention, however, until you reach the Danville road, which I would like you to strike as near to the Appomattox as possible. Make your destruction on that road as complete as possible. You can then pass on to the South Side road, west of Burkesville, and destroy that, in like manner.

"After having accomplished the destruction of the two railroads, which are now the only avenues of supply to Lee's army, you may return to this army, selecting your road further south, or you may go on into North Carolina and join General Sherman. Should you select the latter course, get the information to me as early as possible, so that I may send orders to meet you at Goldsboro'.

"U. S. GRANT, Lieutenant General.

"Major General P. H. SHERIDAN."

On the morning of the 29th the movement commenced. At night the cavalry was at Dinwiddie Court-House, and the left of our infantry line extended to the Quaker road, near its intersection with the Boydton plank road. The position of the troops, from left to right, was as follows: Sheridan, Warren, Humphreys, Ord, Wright, Parke.

Everything looked favorable, to the defeat of the enemy and the capture of Petersburg and Richmond, if the proper effort was made. I therefore addressed the following communication to General Sheridan, having previously informed him verbally not to cut loose for the raid contemplated in his orders until he received notice from me to do so:

"GRAVELLY CREEK, March 29, 1865.

GENERAL: Our line is now unbroken from the Appomattox to Dinwiddie. We are all ready, however, to give up all, from the Jerusalem plank road to Hatcher's run, whenever the forces can be used advantageously. After getting into line south of Hatcher's we pushed forward to find the enemy's position. General Griffin was attacked near where the Quaker road intersects the Boydton road but repulsed it easily, capturing about one hundred men. Humphreys reached Dabney's mill, and was pushing on when last heard from. "I now feel like ending the matter, if it is possible to do so, before going back. I do not want you, therefore, to cut loose and go after the enemy's roads at present. In the morning push around the enemy, if you can, and get on to his right rear. The movements of the enemy's cavalry may, of course, modify your action. We will act all together as one army here until it is seen what can be done with the enemy. The signal officer at Cobb's Hill reported, at 11:30 a.m., that a cavalry column had passed that point from Richmond towards Petersburg, taking forty minutes to pass.

"U. S. GRANT, Lieutenant General.

"Major General P. H. SHERIDAN."

From the night of the 29th to the morning of the 31st the rain fell in such torrents as to make it impossible to move a wheeled vehicle, except as corduroy roads were laid in front of them. During the 30th, Sheridan advanced from Dinwiddie Court-House towards Five Forks, where he found the enemy in force. General Warren advanced and extended his line across the Boydton plank road to near the White Oak road, with a view of getting across the latter; but finding the enemy strong in his front and extending beyond his left, was directed to hold on where he was and fortify. General Humphreys drove the enemy from his front into his main line on the Hatcher, near Burgess's mills. Generals Ord, Wright, and Parke made examinations in their fronts to determine the feasibility of an assault on the enemy's lines. The two latter reported favorably. The enemy confronting us, as he did, at every point from Richmond to our extreme left, I conceived his lines must be weakly held, and could be penetrated if my estimate of his forces was correct. I determined, therefore, to extend my line no further, but to re-enforce General Sheridan with a corps of infantry, and thus enable him to cut loose and turn the enemy's right flank, and with the other corps assault the enemy's lines. The result of the offensive effort of the enemy the week before, when he assaulted Fort Steadman, particularly favored this. The enemy's intrenched picket line captured by us at that time threw the lines occupied by the belligerents so close together at some points that it was but a moment's run from one to the other. Preparations were at once made to relieve General Humphreys' corps, to report to General Sheridan; but the condition of the roads prevented immediate movement. On the morning of the 31st General Warren reported favorably to getting possession of the White Oak road, and was directed to do so. To accomplish this, he moved with one division, instead of his whole corps, which was attacked by the enemy in superior force and driven back on the second division before it had time to form, and it, in turn, forced back upon the third division, when the enemy was checked. A division of the 2d corps was immediately sent to his support, the enemy driven back with heavy loss, and possession of the White Oak road gained. Sheridan advanced, and with a portion of his cavalry got possession of the Five Forks, but the enemy, after the affair with the 5th corps, re-enforced the rebel cavalry, defending that point with infantry, and forced him back towards Dinwiddie Court-House. Here General Sheridan displayed great generalship. Instead of retreating with his whole command on the main army, to tell the story of superior forces encountered, he deployed his cavalry on foot, leaving only mounted men enough to take charge of the horses.

This compelled the enemy to deploy over a vast extent of woods and broken country, and made his progress slow. At this juncture he despatched to me what had taken place, and that he was dropping back slowly on Dinwiddie Court-House. General McKenzie's cavalry and one division of the 5th corps were immediately ordered to his assistance. Soon after, receiving a report from General Meade that Humphreys could hold our position on the Boydton road, and that the other two divisions of the 5th corps could go to Sheridan, they were so ordered at once. Thus the operations of the day necessitated the sending of Warren because of his accessibility, instead of Humphreys, as was intended, and precipitated intended movements. On the morning of the 1st of April, General Sheridan, re-enforced by General Warren, drove the enemy back on Five Forks, where, late in the evening, he assaulted and carried his strongly fortified position, capturing all his artillery and between 5,000 and 6,000 prisoners. About the close of this battle Brevet Major General Charles Griffin relieved Major General Warren in command of the 5th corps. The report of this reached me after nightfall. Some apprehensions filled my mind lest the enemy might desert his lines during the night, and by falling upon General Sheridan before assistance could reach him, drive him from his position and open the way for retreat. To guard against this, General Miles's division of Humphreys' corps was sent to re-enforce him, and a bombardment was commenced and kept up until 4 o'clock in the morning, (April 2,) when an assault was ordered on the enemy's lines. General Wright penetrated the lines with his whole corps, sweeping everything before him and to his left towards Hatcher's Run, capturing many guns and several thousand prisoners. He was closely followed by two divisions of General Ord's command, until he met the other division of General

Ord's that had succeeded in forcing the enemy's lines near Hatcher's Run. Generals Wright and Ord immediately swung to the right, and closed all of the enemy on that side of them in Petersburg, while General Humphreys pushed forward with two divisions and joined General Wright on the left. General Parke succeeded in carrying the enemy's main line, capturing guns and prisoners, but was unable to carry his inner line. General Sheridan being advised of the condition of affairs, returned General Miles to his proper command. On reaching the enemy's lines immediately surrounding Petersburg, a portion of General Gibbon's corps, by a most gallant charge, captured two strong, enclosed works – the most salient and commanding south of Petersburg – thus materially shortening the line of investment necessary for taking in the city. The enemy south of Hatcher's Run retreated, westward to Sutherland's Station, where they were overtaken by Miles's division. A severe engagement ensued and lasted until both his right and left flanks were threatened by the approach of General Sheridan, who was moving from Ford's Station towards Petersburg, and a division sent by General Meade from the front of Petersburg, when he broke in the utmost confusion, leaving in our hands his guns and many prisoners. This force retreated by the main road along the Appomattox river. During the night of the 2d the enemy evacuated Petersburg and Richmond, and retreated toward Danville. On the morning of the 3d pursuit was commenced. General Sheridan pushed for the Danville road, keeping near the Appomattox, followed by General Meade with the 2d and 6th corps, while General Ord moved for Burkesville along the South Side road; the 9th corps stretched along that road behind him. On the 4th General Sheridan struck the Danville road near Jettersville, where he learned that Lee was at Amelia Court-House. He immediately intrenched himself and awaited the arrival of General Meade, who reached there the next day. General Ord reached Burkesville on the evening of the 5th.

On the morning of the 5th I addressed Major General Sherman the following communication:

"WILSON'S STATION, April 5, 1865

"GENERAL: All indications now are that Lee will attempt to reach Danville with the remnant of his force. Sheridan, who was up with him last night, reports all that is left, horse, foot, and dragoons, at 20,000, much demoralized. We hope to reduce this number one-half. I shall push on to Burkesville, and if a stand is made at Danville, will in a very few days go there. If you can possibly do so, push on from where you are, and let us see if we cannot finish the job with Lee's and Johnston's armies. Whether it will be better for you to strike for Greensboro', or nearer to Danville, you will be better able to judge when you receive this. Rebel armies now are the only strategic points to strike at.

"U. S. GRANT, Lieutenant General.

"Major General W. T. SHERMAN."

On the morning of the 6th it was found that General Lee was moving west of Jettersville, towards Danville. General Sheridan moved with his cavalry, (the 5th corps having been returned to General Meade on his reaching Jettersville,) to strike his flank, followed by the 6th corps, while the 2d and 5th corps pressed hard after, forcing him to abandon several hundred wagons and several pieces of artillery. General Ord advanced from Burkesville toward

Farmville, sending two regiments of infantry and a squadron of cavalry, under Brevet Brigadier General Theodore Read, to reach and destroy the bridges. This advance met the head of Lee's column near Farmville, which it heroically attacked and detained until General Read was killed and his small force overpowered. This caused a delay in the enemy's movements, and enabled General Ord to get well up with the remainder of his force, on meeting which the enemy immediately intrenched himself. In the afternoon General Sheridan struck the enemy south of Sailor's creek, captured 16 pieces of artillery, and about 400 wagons, and detained him until the 6th corps got up, when a general attack of infantry and cavalry was made, which resulted in the capture of 6,000 or 7,000 prisoners, among whom were many general officers. The movements of the 2d corps and General Ord's command contributed greatly to the day's success.

On the morning of the 7th the pursuit was renewed, the cavalry, except one division, and the 5th corps moving by Prince Edward's Court-House; the 6th corps, General Ord's command, and one division of cavalry, on Farmville, and the 2d corps by the High Bridge road. It was soon found that the enemy had crossed to the north side of the Appomattox; but so close was the pursuit that the 2d corps got possession of the common bridge at High Bridge before the enemy could destroy it, and immediately crossed over. The 6th corps and a division of cavalry crossed at Farmville to its support.

Feeling now that General Lee's chance of escape was utterly hopeless, I addressed him the following communication from Farmville:

"APRIL 7, 1865.

"GENERAL: The result of the last week must convince you of the hopelessness of further resistance on the part of the army of northern Virginia in this struggle. I feel that it is so, and regard it as my duty to shift from myself the responsibility of any further effusion of blood by asking of you the surrender of that portion of the Confederate States army known as the army of northern Virginia.

"U. S. GRANT, Lieutenant General.

"General R. E. LEE."

Early on the morning of the 8th, before leaving, I received, at Farmville, the following:

"APRIL 7, 1865.

"GENERAL: I have received your note of this date. Though not entertaining the opinion you express on the hopelessness of further resistance on the part of the army of northern Virginia, I reciprocate your desire to avoid useless effusion of blood, and therefore, before considering your proposition, ask the terms you will offer on condition of its surrender.

"R. E. LEE, General.

"Lieutenant General U. S. GRANT."
To this I immediately replied:

"APRIL 8, 1865.

"GENERAL: Your note of last evening, in reply to mine on same date, asking the condition on which I will accept the surrender of the army of northern Virginia, is just received. In reply, I would say that peace being my great desire, there is but one condition I would insist upon, namely: that the men and officers surrendered shall be disqualified for taking up arms again against the government of the United States until properly exchanged. I will meet you, or will designate officers to meet any officers you may name for the same purpose, at any point agreeable to you, for the purpose of arranging definitely the terms upon which the surrender of the army of northern Virginia will be received.

"U. S. GRANT, Lieutenant General.

"General R. E. LEE."

Early on the morning of the 8th the pursuit was resumed. General Meade followed north of the Appomattox, and General Sheridan, with all the cavalry, pushed straight for Appomattox Station, followed by General Ord's command and the 5th corps. During the day General Meade's advance had considerable fighting with the enemy's rear guard, but was unable to bring on a general engagement. Late in the evening General Sheridan struck the railroad at Appomattox Station, drove the enemy from there, and captured 25 pieces of artillery, a hospital train, and four trains of cars loaded with supplies for Lee's army. During this day I accompanied General Meade's column, and about midnight received the following communication from General Lee:

"APRIL 8, 1865.

"GENERAL: I received at a late hour your note of today. In mine of yesterday I did not intend to propose the surrender of the army of northern Virginia, but to ask the terms of your proposition. To be frank, I do not think the emergency has arisen to call for the surrender of this army, but as the restoration of peace should be the sole object of all, I desired to know whether your proposals would lead to that end. I cannot, therefore, meet you with a view to surrender the army of northern Virginia, but as far as your proposal may affect the Confederate States forces under my command, and tend to the restoration of peace, I should be pleased to meet you at 10 a.m., tomorrow, on the old stage road to Richmond, between the picket lines of the two armies.

"R. E. LEE, General.

"Lieutenant General U. S. GRANT."

Early on the morning of the 9th I returned him an answer as follows, and immediately started to join the column south of the Appomattox:

"APRIL 9, 1865.

"GENERAL: Your note of yesterday is received. I have no authority to treat on the subject of peace; the meeting proposed for 10 a.m. to-day could lead to no good. I will state, however, general, that I am equally anxious for peace with yourself, and the whole north entertains the same feeling. The terms upon which peace can be had are well understood. By the south laying down their arms they will hasten that most desirable event, save thousands of human lives, and hundreds of millions of property not yet destroyed. Seriously hoping that all our difficulties may be settled without the loss of another life, I subscribe myself, &c.,

"U. S. GRANT, Lieutenant General.

"General R. E. LEE."

On the morning of the 9th General Ord's command and the 5th corps reached Appomattox Station just as the enemy was making a desperate effort to break through our cavalry. The infantry was at once thrown in. Soon after a white flag was received, requesting a suspension of hostilities pending negotiations for a surrender.

Before reaching General Sheridan's headquarters, I received the following from General Lee:

"APRIL 9, 1865.

"GENERAL: I received your note of this morning on the picket line, whither I had come to meet you, and ascertain definitely what terms were embraced in your proposal of yesterday with reference to the surrender of this army. I now ask an interview in accordance with the offer contained in your letter of yesterday for that purpose.

"R. E. LEE, General.

"Lieutenant General U. S. GRANT."

The interview was held at Appomattox Court-House, the result of which is set forth in the following correspondence:

"APPOMATTOX COURT-HOUSE, VA., April 9, 1865.

"GENERAL: In accordance with the substance of my letter to you of the 8th instant, I propose to receive the surrender of the army of northern Virginia on the following terms, to-wit: Rolls of all the officers and men to be made in duplicate, one copy to be given to an officer to be designated by me, the other to be retained by such officer or officers as you may designate. The officers to give their individual paroles not to take up arms against the government of the United States until properly exchanged; and each company or regimental commander sign a like parole for the men of their commands. The arms, artillery, and public property to be parked and stacked, and turned over to the officers appointed by me to receive them. This will not embrace the side-arms of the officers nor their private horses or baggage. This done, each officer and man will be allowed to return to his home, not to be disturbed by United States authority so long as they observe their paroles and the laws in force where they may reside.

"U. S. GRANT, Lieutenant General.

"General R. E. LEE."

"HEADQUARTERS ARMY OF NORTHERN VIRGINIA,

April 9, 1865.

"GENERAL: I received your letter of this date containing the terms of the surrender of the army of northern Virginia as proposed by you. As they are substantially the same as those expressed in your letter of the 8th instant, they are accepted. I will proceed to designate the proper officers to carry the stipulations into effect.

R. E. LEE, General.

"Lieutenant General U. S. GRANT."

The command of Major General Gibbon, the 5th army corps under Griffin, and McKenzie's cavalry, were designated to remain at Appomattox Court-House until the paroling of the surrendered army was completed, and to take charge of the public property. The remainder of the army immediately returned to the vicinity of Burkesville.

General Lee's great influence throughout the whole south caused his example to be followed, and today the result is that the armies lately under his leadership are at their homes, desiring peace and quiet, and their arms are in the hands of our ordnance officers.

On the receipt of my letter of the 5th, General Sherman moved directly against Joe Johnston: who retreated rapidly on and through Raleigh, which place General Sherman occupied on the morning of the 13th. The day preceding news of the surrender of General Lee reached him at Smithfield.

On the 14th a correspondence was opened between General Sherman and General Johnston, which resulted, on the 18th, in an agreement for a suspension of hostilities, and a memorandum or basis for peace, subject to the approval of the President. This agreement was disapproved by the President on the 21st, which disapproval, together with your instructions, was communicated to General Sherman by me in person on the morning of the 24th, at Raleigh, North Carolina, in obedience to your orders. Notice was at once given by him to General Johnston for the termination of the truce that had been entered into. On the 25th another meeting between them was agreed upon, to take place on the 26th, which terminated in the surrender and disbandment of Johnston's army upon substantially the same terms as were given to General Lee.

The expedition under General Stoneman from East Tennessee got off on the 20th of March, moving by way of Boone, North Carolina, and struck the railroad at Wytheville, Chambersburg and Big Lick. The force striking it at Big Lick pushed on to within a few miles of Lynchburg, destroying the important bridges, while with the main force he effectually destroyed it between New river and Big Lick, and then turned for Greensboro' on the North Carolina railroad; struck that road and destroyed the bridges between Danville and Greensboro' and between Greensboro' and the Yadkin, together with the depots of supplies along it, and captured 400 prisoners. At Salisbury he attacked and defeated a force of the enemy under General Gardiner, capturing 14 pieces of artillery and 1,364 prisoners, and destroyed large amounts of army stores. At this place he destroyed fifteen miles of railroad and the bridges toward Charlotte. Thence he moved to Slatersville.

General Canby, who had been directed in January to make preparations for a movement from Mobile bay against Mobile and the interior of Alabama, commenced his movement on the 20th of March. The 16th corps, Major General A. J. Smith commanding, moved from Fort Gaines by water to Fish river; the 13th corps, under Major General Gordon Granger, moved from Fort Morgan and joined the 16th corps on Fish river, both moving thence on Spanish fort and investing it on the 27th; while Major General Steele's command moved from Pensacola, cut the railroad leading from Texas to Montgomery, effected a junction with them, and partially invested Fort Blakely. After a severe bombardment of Spanish fort, a part of its line was carried on the 8th of April. During the night the enemy evacuated the fort. Fort Blakely was carried by assault on the 9th, and many prisoners captured; our loss was considerable. These successes practically opened to us the Alabama river, and enabled us to approach Mobile from the north. On the night of the 11th the city was evacuated, and was taken possession of by our forces on the morning of the 12th.

The expedition under command of Brevet Major General Wilson, consisting of twelve thousand five hundred mounted men, was delayed by rains until March 22, when it moved from Chickasaw, Alabama. On the 1st of April General Wilson encountered the enemy in force under Forrest near Ebenezer Church, drove him in confusion, captured three hundred prisoners and three guns, and destroyed the central bridge over the Cahawba river. On the 2d he attacked and captured the fortified city of Selma, defended by Forrest with seven thousand men and thirty-two guns, destroyed the arsenal, armory, naval foundry, machine shops, vast quantities of stores, and captured three thousand prisoners. On the 4th he captured and destroyed Tuscaloosa. On the 10th he crossed the Alabama river, and after sending information of his operations to General Canby marched on Montgomery, which place he occupied on the 14th, the enemy having abandoned it. At this place many stores and five steamboats fell into our hands. Thence a force marched direct on Columbus, and another on West Point, both of which places were assaulted and captured on the 16th. At the former place we got fifteen hundred prisoners and fifty-two field-guns, destroyed two gunboats, the navy-yard, foundries, arsenal, many factories, and much other public property. At the latter place we got three hundred prisoners, four guns, and destroyed nineteen locomotives and three hundred cars. On the 20th he took possession of Macon, Georgia, with sixty field-guns, twelve hundred militia, and five generals, surrendered by General Howell Cobb. General Wilson hearing that Jeff Davis was trying to make his escape, sent forces in pursuit, and succeeded in capturing him on the morning of May 11.

On the 4th day of May, General Dick Taylor surrendered to General Canby all the remaining rebel forces east of the Mississippi.

A force sufficient to insure an easy triumph over the enemy under Kirby Smith, west of the Mississippi, was immediately put in motion for Texas, and Major General Sheridan designated for its immediate command; but on the 26th day of May, and before they reached their destination, General Kirby Smith surrendered his entire command to Major General Canby. This surrender did not take place, however, until after the capture of the rebel president and vice-president; and the bad faith was exhibited of first disbanding most of his army and permitting an indiscriminate plunder of public property.

Owing to the report that many of those lately in arms against the government had taken refuge upon the soil of Mexico, carrying with them arms rightfully belonging to the United States, which had been surrendered to us by agreement – among them some of the leaders who had surrendered in person – and the disturbed condition of affairs on the Rio Grande, the orders for troops to proceed to Texas were not changed.

There have been severe combats, raids, expeditions, and movements to defeat the designs and purposes of the enemy, most of them reflecting great credit on our arms, and which contributed greatly to our final triumph, that I have not mentioned. Many of these will be found clearly set forth in the reports herewith submitted; some in the telegrams and brief despatches announcing them, and others, I regret to say, have not as yet been officially reported.

For information touching our Indian difficulties, I would respectfully refer to the reports of the commanders of departments in which they have occurred.

It has been my fortune to see the armies of both the west and the east fight battles, and from what I have seen I know there is no difference in their fighting qualities. All that it was possible for men to do in battle they have done. The western armies commenced their battles in the Mississippi valley, and received the final surrender of the remnant of the principal army opposed to them in North Carolina. The armies of the east commenced their battles on the river from which the army of the Potomac derived its name, and received the final surrender of their old antagonist at Appomattox Court-House, Virginia. The splendid achievements of each have nationalized our victories, removed all sectional jealousies, (of which we have unfortunately experienced too much,) and the cause of crimination and recrimination that might have followed had either section failed in its duty. All have a proud record, and all sections can well congratulate themselves and each other for having done their full share in restoring the supremacy of law over every foot of territory belonging to the United States. Let them hope for perpetual peace and harmony with that enemy, whose manhood, however mistaken the cause, drew forth such herculean deeds of valor.

I have the honor to be, very respectfully, your obedient servant,

U. S. GRANT,
Lieutenant General.

Hon. E. M. STANTON,
 Secretary of War.

Lt. General U.S. Grant

Official copy.

ADJUTANT GENERAL'S OFFICE,
November 18, 1865.

E. D. TOWNSEND,
Assistant Adjutant General.